MW00343955

Fourth Edition

IEPs: Guide to Writing Individualized Education Programs

Fourth Edition

IEPs: Guide to Writing Individualized Education Programs

Gordon S. Gibb
Brigham Young University

Tina M. Taylor
Brigham Young University

 Pearson

Please contact https://support.pearson.com/getsupport/s/contactsupport with any queries on this content

Copyright © 2022, 2016, 2007 Pearson Education, Inc. 221 River Street, Hoboken, NJ 07030. All Rights Reserved. Manufactured in the United States of America. This publication is protected by copyright, and permission should be obtained from the publisher prior to any prohibited reproduction, storage in a retrieval system, or transmission in any form or by any means, electronic, mechanical, photocopying, recording, or otherwise. For information regarding permissions, request forms, and the appropriate contacts within the Pearson Education Global Rights and Permissions department, please visit www.pearsoned .com/permissions/.

Acknowledgments of third-party content appear on the appropriate page within the text.
Cover Image Credit: FS Productions/Getty Images

PEARSON, ALWAYS LEARNING, and MYLAB are exclusive trademarks owned by Pearson Education, Inc. or its affiliates in the U.S. and/or other countries.

Unless otherwise indicated herein, any third-party trademarks, logos, or icons that may appear in this work are the property of their respective owners, and any references to third-party trademarks, logos, icons, or other trade dress are for demonstrative or descriptive purposes only. Such references are not intended to imply any sponsorship, endorsement, authorization, or promotion of Pearson's products by the owners of such marks, or any relationship between the owner and Pearson Education, Inc., or its affiliates, authors, licensees, or distributors.

Library of Congress Cataloging-in-Publication Data
Names: Gibb, Gordon S., author. | Taylor, Tina, author.
Title: IEPs : guide to writing individualized education programs / Gordon S. Gibb, Brigham Young University, Tina Taylor, Brigham Young University.
Description: Fourth edition. | Hoboken : Pearson, [2022] | Revised edition of: IEPs : writing quality individualized education programs. | Includes bibliographical references. | Summary: "The author designed this guide for anyone involved in the special education of students with disabilities. It is useful for parents, pre-service and in-service education professionals, and others who support families or provide services to these students. We know that many of you regularly serve, or will serve, on teams that provide educational services to students with disabilities, and you will likely be responsible for contributing to the development of Individualized Education Programs (IEPs). This guide will facilitate your collaborative work on these teams"--Provided by publisher.
Identifiers: LCCN 2020029505 | ISBN 9780135915783 (paperback) | ISBN 9780135915769 | ISBN 9780135915820 (ebook)
Subjects: LCSH: Individualized education programs. | Special education.
Classification: LCC LC4019 .G52 2022 | DDC 371.9/04394--dc23
LC record available at https://lccn.loc.gov/2020029505

9 2022

Print Book:
ISBN 10: 0-13-591578-3
ISBN 13: 978-0-13-591578-3

Instructor's Review Copy:
ISBN 10: 0-13-680089-0
ISBN 13: 978-0-13-680089-7

Table of Contents

Preface

WELCOME TO IEPS: GUIDE TO WRITING INDIVIDUALIZED EDUCATION PROGRAMS, 4TH EDITION

We designed this guide for anyone involved in the special education of students with disabilities. It is useful for parents, preservice and inservice education professionals, and others who support families or provide services to these students. We know that many of you regularly serve, or will serve, on teams that provide educational services to students with disabilities, and you will likely be responsible for contributing to the development of Individualized Education Programs (IEPs). This guide will facilitate your collaborative work on these teams.

Our goal is to help you write quality IEPs. Because the IEP is a legal document that guides the education of students with disabilities, it is critical that you gain the skills and knowledge to create IEPs that meet the standards of the law. To help you gain a deeper understanding of this process, we have organized this guide with several helpful features:

- Summary of IDEA 2004 in language that is easy to understand
- Organization of the IEP process into seven manageable steps
- Explanation, modeling, practice, and feedback for each step
- Brief procedural summary at the end of each step
- Emphasis on standards-based IEPs aligned with core curricula
- Writing standards-based goals for students achieving well below grade level
- Role of Response to Intervention (RTI) and Multi-Tiered Systems of Supports (MTSS)
- A personal guide, My Mentor, to provide comments, directions, and suggestions as you read and complete each step in the guide

We have also added several new features:

- New cases and sample IEPs for four students with varying disabilities, ages, and family circumstances, including transition planning in Meet Our Students.
- Further modeling and guidance for writing present levels of academic achievement and functional performance (PLAAFP) statements in Step 1.
- Expanded section on measuring progress toward IEP goals with examples in Step 3.
- Additional detail about how to discuss and address least restrictive environment in IEP meetings in Step 4.
- Impact of the *Endrew F. v. Douglas County School District* Supreme Court decision in Step 2.
- Alignment with the requirements of the *Every Student Succeeds Act* throughout the book.
- Improved and expanded chapter on transition planning in Step 7.

ASSUMPTIONS BEHIND THIS GUIDE

In developing this guide, we have assumed that you and the rest of the school team have completed the identification, referral, evaluation, and classification processes for your students with disabilities. This guide begins at the point when your team is ready to develop students' IEPs.

PARAMETERS FOR THIS GUIDE

This guide does not address planning for students without disabilities who struggle in school. Students whose primary language is not English; or whose learning difficulties are caused by environmental, cultural, or economic disadvantages; or who have not received appropriate instruction are not eligible for special education and, therefore, do not need an IEP unless they also have a disability. These students may be served by other programs such as bilingual education, Title 1, or Section 504 of the Rehabilitation Act of 1973.

LEGAL BASIS FOR THIS GUIDE

Federal law mandates the special education process, so we have structured this guide in accordance with federal law and regulations, and we use terminology from the federal law throughout the text. Individual states must meet the requirements of the federal law but may also add specific state policies and procedures. You should consult your state and district regulations for their specific policies, procedures, and terminology.

ACKNOWLEDGMENTS

We express our gratitude to Sharon Black for her excellent editing/proofreading and to Drew Bennett, Rebecca Fox-Gieg, Bridget Daly, and Janelle Rogers at Pearson for their patient support of our efforts in completing this fourth edition.

—GSG and TMT

About the Authors

Gordon S. Gibb, PhD, taught students with disabilities in the public schools for 16 years prior to his appointment at Brigham Young University in 1995. Dr. Gibb prepared teacher candidates to work with students with mild/moderate disabilities and conducted instructional improvement activities in schools and college. His research centers on cultural models for understanding disability and on effective instruction for individuals with disabilities at several levels. Dr. Gibb likes teaching, woodworking, family history, grandchildren, and the outdoors. He retired in 2019.

Tina Taylor, EdD, is a professor and associate dean in the McKay School of Education at Brigham Young University. Dr. Taylor has worked with individuals with significant disabilities and their families for over 30 years as a special educator and professor. Her service and research interests include adaptation of families raising children with disabilities, children's literature that characterizes individuals with disabilities, and provision of appropriate services to individuals with disabilities. Dr. Taylor enjoys spending time with family, playing sports, traveling, and reading.

Introduction: Special Education and the Individualized Education Program

Judy Heumann, the daughter of Jewish immigrants from Germany who settled in Brooklyn in 1947, had polio when she was about 18-months-old. The little girl, who was unable to walk and relied on a wheelchair, participated in her local Brownies club and later went to summer camps. But when it came time to go to school, Heumann discovered her East Flatbush community had no place for her. She had to make do with a teacher who came to the house to give her lessons.

"Having grown up in Brooklyn when there were no laws for disabled people, I was denied my right to go to my neighborhood school; it was not wheelchair accessible and I got only 2.5 hours of education a week until the 4th grade," Heumann said (Otis, 2015, paras. 8, 10, 12–14).

Judy's experience typifies the lack of public school opportunities for American children and youth with disabilities until late in the 20th century. Prior to 1975, there was no universally applicable law that required states or schools to help these children learn. In 1970, only one in five children with disabilities received schooling, and some states specifically excluded children with certain disabilities from attending public schools (Office of Special Education Programs, 2000). Reasons for exclusion included inconvenience to school personnel, lack of teacher expertise, and fears of other children being adversely affected by associating with children with disabilities. Many individuals with disabilities were housed in institutions, often with minimal care and insufficient food, clothing, and shelter (Office of Special Education Programs, 2000). Fortunately, the tide of civil rights legislation in the 1950s and 60s, along with increased public advocacy and a series of pivotal legal decisions, moved Congress to pass the *Education for all Handicapped Children Act* in 1975, mandating free and appropriate public education for all children, regardless of disability. The 2004 *Individuals with Disabilities Education Improvement Act* (IDEA), the current version of this landmark law, governs special education in the United States. Judy Heumann, who as a child was denied a free and appropriate public education, became a lifelong disability rights advocate and officer in the U.S. Department of Education. She was instrumental in developing legislation that became IDEA.

WHO ARE STUDENTS WITH DISABILITIES?

IDEA states that students with disabilities are those who experience developmental delays (ages 3–9) or are classified by their multidisciplinary team as having one of these 12 disabilities:

- Autism
- Deaf-blindness
- Hearing impairment, including deafness
- Intellectual disabilities
- Multiple disabilities
- Orthopedic impairment
- Other health impairment
- Serious emotional disturbance
- Specific learning disabilities
- Speech or language impairment
- Traumatic brain injury
- Visual impairment, including blindness

WHAT IS SPECIAL EDUCATION?

IDEA defines special education as

> Specially designed instruction, at no cost to parents, to meet the unique needs of a student with a disability, including instruction conducted in the classroom, in the home, in hospitals and institutions, and in other settings; and instruction in physical education. (34 CFR §300.39)

Special education is not a place, like a resource room or self-contained classroom, but is "specially designed instruction" provided in whatever setting the IEP team determines is appropriate. To provide special education, each state must assure that all students ages 3–21 with disabilities who reside in the state have access to five provisions:

1. Free appropriate public education
2. Nondiscriminatory evaluation
3. Individualized education program
4. Least restrictive environment
5. Procedural safeguards

The statements below are quoted directly from the referenced sections of the law.

1. **Free Appropriate Public Education.** This is defined as special education and related services that
   - are provided to students with disabilities at public expense, under public supervision, and without charge;
   - meet the standards of the state educational agency;
   - include appropriate preschool, elementary school, or secondary school education; and
   - are provided consistent with each student's individualized education program. (34 CFR §300.17)

2. **Nondiscriminatory Evaluation.** To serve a student in special education, a school must first conduct an evaluation to determine if the student has a disability, if the disability inhibits progress in the general curriculum, and if special education is needed to meet the student's individual needs. This evaluation must use a variety of assessment tools and strategies to gather relevant functional, developmental, and academic information to determine if a student has a disability and to assist in determining the content of the IEP. The evaluation should include information about the student provided by the parent. For the evaluation to be nondiscriminatory it should
   - avoid relying on any single measure or assessment to determine if a student has a disability;
   - use technically sound instruments that may assess the relative contribution of cognitive and behavioral factors, in addition to physical or developmental factors;
   - be selected and administered with care to avoid racial or cultural discrimination;
   - be provided and administered in the language and communication form most likely to yield accurate information on what the student knows and can do academically, developmentally, and functionally, unless this is not feasible;
   - use instruments that are valid and reliable, administered by trained and knowledgeable personnel;
   - assess the student in all areas of suspected disability; and
   - allow for coordination between schools for students who transfer from one agency to another in the same academic year. (34 CFR §300.304)

3. **Individualized Education Program.** If the results of the evaluation indicate that a student needs special education, then an individualized education program (IEP) must be developed. The IEP, developed by a team, is a document that includes the following:
   - A statement of the student's **present levels of academic achievement and functional performance**, including
     - how the disability affects the student's involvement and progress in the general education curriculum; or
     - for preschool students, how the disability affects participation in appropriate activities.

- A statement of **measurable annual goals**, including academic and functional goals, designed to
  - meet the student's needs that result from the disability, enabling the student to be involved in and make progress in the general curriculum; and
  - meet each of the student's other educational needs that result from the disability;
  - for students who take alternate assessments aligned with alternate achievement standards, a description of benchmarks or short-term objectives.
- A description of how the **student's progress** toward meeting the annual goals will be measured and when periodic reports on the student's progress will be provided.
- A statement of the **special education, related services, and supplementary aids and services**, based on peer-reviewed research to the extent practicable, to be provided to the student
  - to advance toward attaining the annual goals;
  - to be involved in and make progress in the general education curriculum; and
  - to participate in extracurricular and other nonacademic activities.
- An explanation of the extent, if any, to which the **student will not participate** with nondisabled students in the regular class and in extracurricular and other nonacademic activities
- A statement of any individual appropriate **accommodations** that are necessary to measure the academic achievement and functional performance of the student on state and district-wide assessments, and if the IEP Team determines that the student shall take an alternate assessment, explanations of
  - why the student cannot participate in the regular assessment, and
  - which alternate assessment has been selected as appropriate for the student.
- The **projected date** for the beginning of the IEP and the anticipated frequency, location, and duration of the services and modifications
- A **transition plan** beginning not later than the first IEP to be in effect when the student is 16, and updated annually thereafter, including
  - appropriate measurable post-secondary goals based upon age-appropriate transition assessments related to training, education, employment, and, where appropriate, independent living skills,
  - the transition services, including courses of study, needed to assist the student in reaching those goals, and
  - beginning not later than one year before the student reaches the age of majority under state law, a statement that the student has been informed of the rights that will transfer to him or her on reaching the age of majority. (34 CFR §300.320)

4. **Least Restrictive Environment.** This means that students with disabilities will be educated with students without disabilities to the maximum extent appropriate. These learning environments include public or private institutions or other

care facilities. Special classes, separate schooling, or other removal of students with disabilities from the regular educational environment occurs only when the nature or severity of a student's disability is such that education in regular classes with the use of supplementary aids and services cannot be achieved satisfactorily. (34 CFR §300.114)

What does "Maximum Extent Appropriate" mean? Note the wording is "maximum extent *appropriate*" rather than "maximum extent possible." This means that the IEP team determines the appropriate learning environment(s) to meet each student's needs but does not insist on full inclusion in the general education classroom if this placement would not meet the student's needs.

5. **Procedural Safeguards.** Schools must establish and maintain procedures to ensure that students with disabilities and their parents are guaranteed procedural safeguards as a free appropriate public education is provided. A document explaining these procedural safeguards or "parents' rights" must be given to parents annually, typically at or before the IEP meeting. The document must be in the native language of the parents, unless use of this language is clearly not feasible, and must be written in an easily understandable style. The document must include a full explanation of the following safeguards:

- Parents may present information from an independent educational evaluation to be considered in determining the existence of a disability and/or designating the contents of the IEP.
- Parents must be provided with written notice and provide written consent before any action is taken with regard to the education of their child with a disability.
- Parents have access to their child's educational records.
- Parents have the opportunity to present and participate in resolving complaints through mediation or due process.
- Parents should receive an explanation of the procedures for due process hearings.
- Parents have the right to keep their child in the current placement pending and during a due process hearing.
- Parents should receive an explanation of procedures for students who are subject to placement in an interim alternative educational setting.
- Parents should be provided an explanation of the requirements for unilateral placement parents may make of students in private schools at public expense.
- Parents should receive an explanation of state-level appeals.
- Parents should receive an explanation of procedures for civil actions.
- Parents should receive an explanation of attorney's fees. (34 CFR §300.500-536)

These five principles have been important aspects of special education since the first law was passed in 1975. The requirements for each principle have been altered somewhat in subsequent reauthorizations of IDEA, but the basic framework of special education in the United States has remained the same. Now that you know the legal requirements for providing special education, you should understand how the process begins and what it involves.

HOW DOES THE SPECIAL EDUCATION PROCESS BEGIN?

The special education process begins when parents or a teacher makes a formal referral for evaluation to determine if a child has a disability. If the disability was evident before or soon after the child was born or during the preschool years, parents make the referral. But most disabilities are identified after a student does not achieve as expected in school.

When the classroom teacher's efforts to provide interventions for a struggling child are not successful at meeting the child's needs, the teacher can initiate a referral to determine if the student has a disability. The teacher must provide evidence that the child has participated in scientific, research-based interventions to address his or her individual needs, including data about the student's response to the interventions. If the multidisciplinary team's assessment indicates that the student has a disability and is eligible for special education services, then an IEP is developed.

WHAT IS THE ROLE OF THE IEP IN SPECIAL EDUCATION?

The IEP is a legal document with two essential roles. First, it is the individualized component of special education planning, defining what *appropriate* means in the specific student's free appropriate public education. The IEP describes a student's special education program for one year, including goals for improvement and ways the school will help the student achieve the goals. The IEP emphasizes ways to help the student make progress in the general curriculum and participate along with peers without

Response to Intervention

Response to Intervention (RTI) is a school-wide approach to meeting students' needs based on how well they respond to various levels of instruction. Figure 1 depicts a **multi-tiered system of supports** for academic and behavioral needs, focusing first on the general classroom and moving to more intensive support in smaller groups as needed. RTI is an excellent way to ensure that students receive appropriate research-based interventions, which may meet their needs without referral for special education services.

FIGURE 1 Response to intervention (RTI).

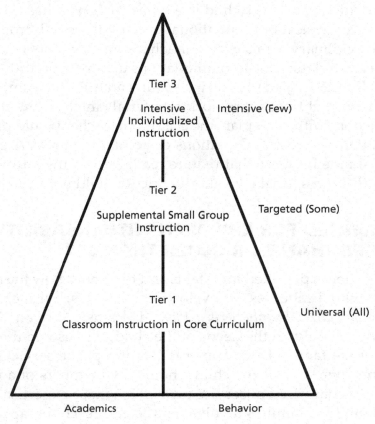

Tier 3

Intensive
Individualized
Instruction

Intensive (Few)

Tier 2

Supplemental Small Group
Instruction

Targeted (Some)

Tier 1

Classroom Instruction in Core Curriculum

Universal (All)

Academics   Behavior

disabilities in extracurricular activities of an appropriate nature and extent. The IEP might be viewed as a personal roadmap for a student's education and extracurricular activities.

Second, the IEP serves as a basis for communication between parents and teachers regarding the student's educational growth and achievement. When parents and teachers both know the goals for the student's improvement, they have common reference points for discussion and decisions.

WHO NEEDS AN IEP?

Any student between the ages of 3 and 21 who receives special education services must have a current IEP. To verify that a student is eligible for special education, three questions must be answered, with necessary evidence and explanation:

1. Does the student have a disability?
2. Does the disability inhibit progress in the general curriculum?
3. Does the student require specially designed instruction to progress in the general curriculum?

Some students have disabilities that do not significantly impact their progress in the general curriculum, such as a child in a wheelchair who has no problem learning and does not need physical or occupational therapy to benefit from the general curriculum. Multidisciplinary teams determine that some students who have disabilities are eligible to receive classroom accommodations under Section 504 of the Rehabilitation Act of 1973 (29 U.S.C. §701) but do not require an IEP. For example, a student with visual impairment might need large-print materials in class, but not need specially designed instruction. With a 504 plan, the classroom teacher would provide large-print materials and other necessary adaptations or accommodations (e.g., front-row seating or additional time for tasks that require reading), but the multidisciplinary team decides that an IEP and special education services would not be required.

ARE IEPS CREATED FOR CHILDREN WITH DISABILITIES WHO ARE YOUNGER THAN 3 OR OLDER THAN 21?

No. Special education is provided for infants and toddlers below the age of 3 who have been diagnosed with disabilities or developmental delays, but such interventions are based on an *Individualized Family Service Plan* (IFSP) instead of an IEP (USC §34.636). The IFSP focuses not only on the needs of the child, but also on the concerns, needs, and resources of the family. Developmentally appropriate services are provided in natural environments, such as the child's home, by members of a multidisciplinary team. This team is comprised of service providers whose expertise is needed for the child's progress and the family's involvement (e.g., speech therapist, physical therapist, social worker, program coordinator). The IFSP facilitates the child's transition to preschool or other services or discontinues special education services that are no longer needed.

Adults with disabilities are not eligible for special education services after their 22nd birthday; therefore, these individuals do not have IEPs. From this age, individuals who still need services must depend on family or community support or on government agencies to meet their needs. Unfortunately, there is no guarantee that services will be available for all adults with disabilities who need them. Availability of services for adults with disabilities varies greatly across the United States.

WHO DEVELOPS THE IEP?

The IEP is developed by a team—often called the IEP team or the multidisciplinary team—that meets and discusses relevant information about the student's strengths and needs. IDEA states that the IEP team must consist of these members:

- The parents of the student with a disability
- At least one regular education teacher of the student if the student is or may be participating in the regular class
- At least one special education teacher or one special education provider

- A representative of the local education agency (LEA), usually the principal, who is qualified to provide or supervise the provision of special education for the student, is knowledgeable about the general education curriculum, and is knowledgeable about the availability of resources
- An individual who can interpret evaluation results, possibly one of those already mentioned on this list, such as a school psychologist
- At the discretion of the parent or school, other individuals who have knowledge or special expertise regarding the student, such as a speech-language pathologist or a physical therapist
- Whenever appropriate, the student with a disability (34 CFR §300.321)

Please remember that each member of the IEP team contributes unique and essential information. Parents may be intimidated by the IEP process or may feel less qualified than the professionals on the team; however, parents know their children better than anyone else does. The team should seek and value parental input throughout the IEP process.

HOW DO I WORK WITH CULTURALLY AND LINGUISTICALLY DIVERSE STUDENTS AND THEIR FAMILIES IN THE IEP PROCESS?

Culturally and linguistically diverse (CLD) students and their families have particular needs that should be addressed throughout the IEP process. The team should understand families' experiences and values related to education and use this understanding as they identify and evaluate the disability, develop the IEP, and make decisions regarding placement and service provision for the child.

Though the number of CLD students increases annually, a vast majority of public school teachers in the United States are white females (U.S. Department of Education, 2018). Understanding the students' family and cultural contexts will help the team alleviate some of the risk factors related to dropping out of school, failing to graduate, and being inappropriately referred for special education. However, educators should avoid viewing cultural differences as general lists of behaviors or attitudes that members of groups invariably adopt (Ford, 2016). Instead, cultural practices within families are fluid, hybrid, and dynamic. Understanding cultural differences in terms of daily activities and practices is critical to understand and serve students (Weisner, 2014).

Many resources provide helpful suggestions for serving CLD students with disabilities. Following are a few points to consider:

- During the evaluation process, be aware that standardized assessment processes and tools may not be designed for use with CLD students.
- Consider contextual factors such as the values, behaviors, and beliefs of the student and his or her family, particularly in the classification process; people from various backgrounds and cultures do not necessarily view disability from the same perspectives as school personnel.

- Facilitate participation of CLD parents in the IEP process by reducing barriers caused by language and cultural differences, parents' lack of knowledge about the school system, and parents' fear of being told only what is wrong with their child.
- Consider including a cultural mediator in the IEP meetings (1) to translate the discussion and paperwork for parents who do not speak the language of the school professionals and (2) to clarify possible misunderstandings due to the culture of the school environment compared to that of the student's family.
- Ensure that IEP goals and objectives address both academic and social interaction skills and acknowledge behaviors that are valued in the student's home and community.
- When determining services and education placement, consider the students' need to access instruction in their native language.

Following the IEP meeting, provide parents with information on relevant community resources and offer them opportunities to interact with other CLD parents of children with disabilities.

MY MENTOR
Try to translate and explain concepts and their references to disability, learning, and student benefit in ways parents and others will understand.

Cultural and Linguistic Differences

Terms and concepts do not easily translate from one language or culture to another. For instance, in Mexico *educación* includes being moral; responsible; and a *persona de bien*, or good person; and being loyal to family and traditional values (Gallimore & Goldenberg, 2001). Contrast this with the American concept of education, meaning to have mastered certain skills and content knowledge within an established curriculum. It is not likely that terms used by special educators in the United States will be self-evident when translated for speakers of other languages.

ARE IEPS CREATED ON PAPER OR ON A COMPUTER?

Either. IEPs can be written on paper forms, but schools and districts increasingly use web-based IEP management programs. Several companies offer these subscription programs, which generally require an annual fee and then charge by the number of teachers using the program, the number of IEPs, or both. Most IEP management systems can customize forms for states, districts, or schools for an additional fee. Regardless of the format, all IEPs must contain the information required by law, as outlined in this guide.

WHO HAS ACCESS TO THE IEP?

Only parents and authorized school and district personnel may access a student's IEP and other education records that identify the student. IDEA uses the *Family Educational Rights and Privacy Act* (FERPA) definition of *education records*, which is "records, files, documents, and other materials maintained by an educational agency or institution, or by a person acting for such an agency or institution, that contain information directly related to a student" (20 USC S. 1232g(a)4A). IDEA requires schools to maintain a record of access, available to the public, on which authorized people must record their name, position, date, and reason for accessing confidential materials. Parents may request copies of a student's IEP and other confidential information, as defined by FERPA.

The law's careful description of access rights has two purposes: (1) It defines who can see information which identifies the student, and (2) it informs schools and parents that this information is *confidential,* which means that unauthorized people do not have access to it. For IEP team members, strict confidentiality is required regarding students served by special education. Team members may not disclose such information to others, spoken or written, in or out of school.

Perhaps you have heard an account of a teacher standing in line at a grocery store complaining to a friend about the trials of working with a particular student with a disability. The next person in line was the student's mother, who promptly reported the teacher's breach of confidentiality to the school and district. The lesson from this episode is that teachers must share confidential information *only* with authorized people at appropriate times and in appropriate settings.

HOW DOES THE TEAM PREPARE FOR AN IEP MEETING?

Preparation depends on whether or not the student has an existing IEP. Before referring the child to assess a possible disability, the general classroom teacher attempts to address the student's needs by making adaptations or accommodations in the classroom and documents the student's response, showing that these efforts have not been successful in addressing the student's needs. The student's eligibility for special education is based on the resulting multidisciplinary assessment. If the student is eligible, the team will develop the initial IEP.

Whether or not the IEP is the child's first, the team prepares for the meeting by collecting the formal and informal assessment data that describe the student's present levels of academic achievement and functional performance. The school representatives and the parents set a mutually agreeable time and place to meet, and the school provides the parents with a written prior notice of the meeting. Sometimes school personnel choose to provide parents with a list of potential goals in advance of the meeting and to invite parents to suggest other goals.

WHAT HAPPENS DURING AN IEP MEETING?

Usually the team members meet around a table in a room or office where confidential information can be shared. One of the school professionals conducts the meeting and introduces the participants. If an IEP is currently in place, the team discusses the student's progress toward or achievement of the previous annual goals. The team members then choose whether to continue the existing IEP, to revise it, or to write a new one. The format of IEP meetings may vary among schools and districts, but the general procedures are the same.

Writing IEPs improves with practice, but a set of steps for completing this important process can be useful to beginners. We have been surprised that many IEPs we have seen include the legally required components but are formatted to start at the wrong place in the process: They begin by specifying the services the student will receive instead of by examining the student's current school performance. Thus, teams are inclined to decide special education services before discerning what the student can and needs to do to improve—a classic case of putting the cart before the horse.

WHAT SHOULD THE TEAM DO IF A PARENT CANNOT OR WILL NOT ATTEND THE IEP MEETING?

If a parent cannot attend the meeting, even after good-faith attempts to schedule a mutually agreeable date and time, the law requires the school to use alternative methods of participation, such as video conferencing or conference calls (34 CFR §300.328). If the parent or guardian is unwilling or unable to attend the meeting, the school must maintain a record of its attempts to ensure participation. For example, some districts require the team to send the IEP meeting notice by certified mail so that the mail receipt is a record of the attempt. IDEA also allows the school to email notices if parents choose this option. (34 CFR §300.17)

WHAT HAPPENS IF A TEAM MEMBER DISAGREES WITH THE GROUP DECISIONS FOR THE IEP?

Sometimes a team member or members may disagree with the final version of an IEP. For a parent disagreement with other team members, the law provides a mediation process to address concerns. The school or district must ensure that this process is voluntary for both parties, is conducted by a trained and impartial mediator, and is not used to deny or delay parental rights to further due process. A resolution obtained through mediation must result in a legally binding agreement signed by the disputing parties.

The law also allows the school or district to establish other procedures if the parents choose not to use mediation. This alternate choice involves the use of a third-party dispute resolution entity or a parent training or resource center to explain the benefits of mediation. Parents may then choose whether or not to use mediation to resolve the differences. (34 CFR §300.506)

WHAT IF MEDIATION DOESN'T SOLVE THE PROBLEM?

IDEA guarantees the right of parents or schools to legal due process to resolve disputes relating to a child's identification, evaluation, educational placement, and/or services. Therefore, if mediation does not resolve the concern, parents or schools may request a due process hearing in which legal counsel can call expert witnesses and introduce evidence. A request for due process must be filed within two years of the disputed action. If a due process hearing does not resolve the concern, then both parties have the right to appeal to state or federal courts. (34 CFR §300.507)

 MY MENTOR Due process means that individuals have the right to full protection under the law.

HOW DO TEACHERS AND OTHER SERVICE PROVIDERS USE THE IEP?

Teachers organize instruction to address the IEP goals within the service pattern described while monitoring student progress toward attaining goals in areas affected by the disability. To do this requires teachers and related service providers to carefully plan and implement instruction or intervention and to collect and use data related to student success. For example, a teacher might state this annual goal for math: "Given 20 multiplication and division problems within 100, Sammy will compute and write answers 19/20 correct in one trial." Sammy's teacher must task analyze the goal to determine what concepts and skills are required to achieve it and then design and conduct a sequence of daily lessons to bring Sammy to this level. The challenge is to determine how much can be taught and measured in the time allowed for daily instruction or intervention that will lead to achieving the goal.

HOW ARE IEP PROGRESS DATA COLLECTED AND USED?

Data are collected when teachers or related service providers work from measurable goals or objectives with methods in place to regularly measure student progress. For example, Sammy's teacher should include an assessment of learning for each lesson. If the lesson requires that he compute and write the answer to three multiplication and three matching division problems within 10, then the lesson should include those six items for Sammy to complete during independent practice (see Figure 2). The teacher will record Sammy's score and decide if he has met the mastery criterion. If he has not, more instruction or practice is indicated. Over time the teacher will have a record of the student's progress toward and eventual accomplishment of the annual goal.

FIGURE 2 Assessing Sammy's math learning.

Name: _____	Date: _____

Write the answers to these problems.

$3 \times 3 =$	$2 \times 5 =$	$3 \times 2 =$
$10 \div 5 =$	$9 \div 3 =$	$6 \div 2 =$

Learning target: Compute and write the answer to three multiplication and three matching division problems within 10.

IS IEP PAPERWORK AS TIME-CONSUMING AS I HAVE HEARD IT IS?

The answer could be "yes" or "no." Special education requires more documentation per student served than is required for students without disabilities. Special educators are responsible for complying with federal, state, and district law and policy, and compliance must be documented. Just as important, student achievement data inform instructional decisions.

Just know that your approach to maintaining the required documents helps to determine how much time the process consumes. Efficiency makes the difference. You will save the most time if you complete all required documents correctly and in order *the first time* and keep them in an orderly and accessible storage system.

 Teachers who scramble to put things in order to prepare for an IEP meeting, a program audit, or a compliance review consume much more time than those who establish and follow systematic procedures along the way.

WHAT STEPS ARE INVOLVED IN DEVELOPING AN IEP?

We have outlined seven steps that can lead your team through the process of developing quality IEPs:

1. Describe the student's present levels of academic achievement and functional performance.
2. Write measurable annual goals.
3. Measure and report student progress.
4. State the services needed to achieve annual goals.
5. Explain the extent, if any, to which the student will not participate with nondisabled students in the regular class and in extracurricular and other nonacademic activities.
6. Explain accommodations necessary to measure academic achievement and functional performance on state and district-wide assessments.
7. Complete a transition plan for students aged 16 and older.

When these steps are completed, all IEP team members confirm their participation in the meeting by signing and dating the IEP.

HOW DOES THE TEAM FOLLOW THE STEPS IN THE IEP PROCESS?

As you learn and practice with this guide, you will find a rationale and explanation for each of the steps so that you can complete the process knowledgeably and professionally. You will also see examples from four case studies of students with disabilities and, where appropriate, counterexamples to guide your learning and help you discriminate between correct and incorrect procedures. Then you will practice each of the steps to check your understanding. As you complete each self-check exercise, compare your answers with our suggested answers in the appendix.

MY MENTOR You are ready to go! Enjoy your learning, and may you find success and fulfillment as you create educational programs for these marvelous children.

References

Family Educational Right to Privacy Act. (1988). 53 FR 11943, 20 USC S. 1232g. http://www.ecfr.gov/cgi-bin/text-idx?c=ecfr&sid=11975031b82001bed902b3e73f3 3e604&rgn=div5&view=text&node=34:1.1.1.1.33&idno=34

Ford, D. Y. (2016). Black and Hispanic students: Cultural differences within the context of education. In L. Corno & E. M. Anderman (Eds.), *Handbook of educational psychology*, (p. 364–377). Routledge/Taylor & Francis Group.

Gallimore, R., & Goldenberg, C. (2001). Analyzing cultural models and settings to connect minority achievement and school improvement research. *Educational Psychologist*, *36*(1), 45–56. https://doi.org/10.1207/S15326985EP3601_5

Office of Special Education Programs. (2000). *Twenty-five years of progress in educating children with disabilities through IDEA*. Washington, D.C. http://www2.ed.gov/policy/speced/leg/idea/history.pdf

Otis, G. A. (2015, July 25). *Trailblazing advocate Judy Heumann says there's more work to do 25 years after Americans with Disabilities Act was signed into law*. New York Daily News. https://www.nydailynews.com/news/national/ada-advocate-judy-heumann-work-article-1.2304397

Rehabilitation Act of 1973. Pub. L. No. 93-112, 87 Stat. 355. 29 U.S.C. §§ 701-796. https://www.eeoc.gov/laws/statutes/rehab.cfm

U.S. Department of Education. (2018). *Digest of education statistics*. Institute of Education Sciences, National Center for Education Statistics. https://nces.ed.gov/programs/coe/indicator_clr.asp

U.S. Department of Education. (2006). Assistance to States for the Education of Children with Disabilities and Preschool Grants for Children with Disabilities; Final Rule, 34 CFR Parts 300, 301, and Part C§636 (2006). www.ed.gov/policy/speced/guid/idea/idea2004.html#law

Weisner, T. S. (2014). Culture, context, and child well-being. In A. Ben-Arieh, F. Casas, I. Frønes, & J. E. Korbin (Eds.), *Handbook of child well-being: Theories, methods and policies in global perspective* (pp. 87–103). Springer.

Meet Our Students

We would like you become acquainted with four students of various ages and types of disabilities, each with a brief biography and an IEP. We believe the biographies remind educators that students are people with their own unique circumstances, not just names on documents. So much of what influences a student's life and learning occurs outside the classroom and the school day; teachers who understand this are more likely to teach the whole child.

The IEPs are examples based on our experience and understanding of the required components described in IDEA. You may notice variations in document formats, indicating that state or district IEPs may differ in appearance or organization while still containing the necessary components.

Our students are

- Phoebe, a seventh-grade girl with serious emotional disturbance living in an urban area;
- Rajesh, a second-grade boy with specific learning disabilities living in an upscale neighborhood;
- Cadence, a nine-year-old girl with intellectual disabilities who learns from an alternate curriculum; and
- Keej, a 19-year-old young man with autism preparing for transition to post-school life.

Phoebe Delacroix

Phoebe is a Caucasian seventh grader attending Barnwell Middle School. Barnwell is a traditional school serving 877 students in grades six through eight in an urban area of the Midwest. The student population is approximately 60% Black, 33% White, and 7% other races, evenly divided between girls and boys. Located in an area of high unemployment and low-income housing, 81% of the school population is economically disadvantaged as measured by the percentage of students qualifying for free and reduced-price meals.

Family and Cultural Background

Phoebe lives with her mother, Amy, and stepmother, Rella, both divorced women who married two years ago. Phoebe has one younger brother and two younger step-sisters, one of whom is a preschooler. Amy is a retail clerk; Rella is recovering from a back injury and has not worked for several months. The family lives in an apartment building within walking distance of the school. They buy their groceries and other daily items at a nearby market and only travel to places that they can reach on foot or by bus.

Amy grew up in a two-parent home with several siblings. She started working out of high school and has not obtained formal post-secondary education. Rella was raised by her alcoholic seldom-employed father and experienced much violence in the home as various live-in girlfriends came and went through the years. She left high school to escape the situation and has held a variety of low-paying unskilled jobs. Neither woman has extended family that can or will provide assistance.

Since Phoebe entered middle school, she has manifested debilitating anxiety that was not evident in elementary school. She does not interact with others outside the home and has a very difficult time attending or remaining in school because of her anxious fears. After several conferences at the school, Amy took the child to a psychologist who diagnosed an anxiety disorder. Amy reported this to the school administrator who suggested formally referring the case to the special education team. Team members completed the evaluation and, referencing the medical report and the impact of her anxiety on her educational progress, determined that Phoebe qualifies for special education services for serious emotional disturbance.

School Experience

Phoebe has always performed at or above grade level in math, reading, and writing. She enrolled in the standard courses for her seventh-grade year but is failing them all. Her anxiety, possibly compounded by the onset of adolescence, has completely overturned her performance and made academic progress unpredictable.

Phoebe goes through cycles of withdrawal during which she stops talking to peers. Withdrawal from peers is followed by withdrawal from teachers as evidenced by sharp decreases in classroom task engagement and attendance. Observations by the school psychologist and two of her classroom teachers over the past month show that Phoebe engages in assigned tasks about 10% of opportunities. She initiates or participates in conversation with peers about 0% of opportunities. Same age and gender peers in her classes engage in tasks 90% of opportunities and initiate or participate in conversations 95% of opportunities.

This year her withdrawal started about the third week of school and lasted until the Thanksgiving break. Phoebe's social and classroom engagement improved somewhat after the break but took a sharp downturn after returning from the December holiday. The IEP team, including Amy, Phoebe, her English teacher, a special educator, the school psychologist, and the principal, met and developed an IEP that they believe will help Phoebe progress. The team is focusing on her interpersonal behaviors with the belief that lessening her classroom anxiety will reduce absenteeism and will improve academic and social/emotional skills.

Individualized Education Program

1. Student Information

Student _Phoebe Delacroix_	3-yr. Re-evaluation _1/21/_	DOB _Aug 16_
School _Barnwell_	IEP Meeting _1/22/_	Classification _Serious emotional disturbance_
IEP Due _1/21/_	Grade _7_	Eligibility Date _1/22/_

2. Present Levels of Academic Achievement and Functional Performance

Behavior   Adult observations on 9/30/__, 10/14/__, 10/27/__, 12/3/__, and 1/22/__ show that Phoebe engages in assigned tasks about 10% of opportunities. She initiates or participates in conversation with peers 0% of opportunities. Same age and gender peers in her classes engage in tasks 90% of opportunities and initiate or participate in conversations 95% of opportunities. To progress in the general curriculum, Phoebe needs to ask for task assistance when needed. To develop appropriate social skills, she needs to participate in peer conversations.

3. The IEP Team considered the following special factors

Behavior	Phoebe needs behavioral strategies because her behavior impedes her learning and social growth.
Language	Not needed.
Braille	Not needed.
Communication	Not needed.
Assistive Technology	Not needed.

4. Measurable Annual Goals

Behavior

1. _Given a new or challenging assignment and without a teacher prompt, Phoebe will ask for help from a peer or adult at least one time for each assignment, 80% of opportunities as measured by adult observation._

2. _When presented with opportunities to interact with peers in small-group settings, Phoebe will initiate conversation and respond to maintain conversation, 80% of opportunities as measured by adult observation._

5. Special Education and Related Services needed to progress in the general curriculum

Special Education Service	Location	Time/Frequency
None		
Related Services		
Behavior intervention .	Classroom	5 hrs/day
	School psychologist office	60 min weekly

Program modifications, supports for school personnel, and/or supplementary aids in the regular education program

School psychologist will consult with general education teachers to teach behavior data collection and behavior reinforcement in the classroom.

6. Participation in State & District Assessment

Participation Codes

S	Standard administration	No accommodations or modifications
A	Participate with accommodations	Does not invalidate, alter, or lower standard
M	Participate with modifications	Invalidates, alters, or lowers standard
AA	Participate using alternate assessment: ☐ Out-of-level Criterion Referenced Tests (CRT) ☐ State alternate assessment	Aligned more closely with alternate curriculum than regular curriculum

	Accommodations	Criterion Referenced Tests			Directed Writing Assessment	State High School Competency Test			Iowa Test of Basic Skills
		Lang Arts	Math	Science		Reading	Writing	Math	
Presentation	1. Direction read aloud in English								
	2. Questions read aloud in English					No			
	3. Directions signed								
	4. Questions signed					No			
	5. Screen reader					No			No
	6. Directions—oral translation								No
	7. Questions—oral translation	No			No	No	No		No
	8. Large print								
	9. Magnification devices								
	10. Braille								
	11. Tactile graphics								
	12. Audio amplification devices								
	13. Visual cues								
	14. Talking materials								
	15. Bilingual word lists	—	—	—	—				No
	16. Translated formulas	—		—	—	—	—		No
Response	17. Word processor—no spell check		—	—				—	—
	18. Calculation devices	—			—	—	—		No
	19. Write in test booklet								
	20. Scribe								
	21. Visual organizers								
	22. Graphic organizers								
	23. Speech-to-text conversion								No
	24. Brailler								
	25. Recording device								

| | Accommodations | Criterion Referenced Tests | | | | State High School Competency Test | | | |
		Lang Arts	Math	Science	Directed Writing Assessment	Reading	Writing	Math	Iowa Test of Basic Skills
Setting	26. Reduce distractions to student								
	27. Reduce distractions to others								
	28. Physical access—ADA								
Timing	29. Extended time								
	30. Multiple breaks								
	31. Schedule change								
Other	32. Other: Temporary (504 only)								

No: Accommodations not allowed   —: Not applicable

7. Regular Curriculum, Extracurricular, and Non-Academic Activities

The student will participate in the regular class, extracurricular, and other nonacademic activities except as noted in special education and related services or listed here: N/A

8. Schedule for Written IEP Progress Reports to Parents

	Weekly	Biweekly	Monthly	Quarterly	Semiannually
Home note		X			
Progress report				X	
Parent conference					X
Report card				X	
Other					

9. Transition Plan (for IEP beginning the year the student turns 16, or before if applicable)

Not applicable

10. Special Requirements for Graduation

Not applicable

11. Notices and Participants

Extended School Year: Extended school year (ESY) services are provided when the team determines the student will not benefit if services are not provided during the normal summer break.

☐ Student is eligible for ESY

☒ Student is not eligible for ESY

Placement Review

Consider the least restrictive environment in which the student will be educated to the maximum extent appropriate with students who do not have disabilities.

Placement Continuum (Pre-K)	Placement Continuum (K–12)	Placement Continuum (Post-Secondary)
☐ Early childhood setting ☐ Early childhood special education ☐ Home ☐ Part-time early childhood/part-time early childhood special education ☐ Public separate school ☐ Private separate school ☐ Public residential facility ☐ Private residential facility ☐ Homebound/hospital	☒ Regular class at least 80% of time ☐ Regular class 40–70% of time ☐ Regular class less than 40% of time ☐ Public separate school ☐ Private separate school ☐ Public residential facility ☐ Private residential facility ☐ Homebound/hospital	☐ Separate classes/program in high school ☐ Off-campus transition program ☐ Transition program on college campus ☐ Public separate school ☐ Private separate school ☐ Public residential facility ☐ Private residential facility ☐ Homebound/hospital

The team determined the student's least restrictive environment:

☒ Initial placement   ☐ Continue placement   ☐ Change placement

IEP Team Participants

Position	Name	Signature	Date
LEA Representative	Eduardo Flores	E.D.Flores	1/22/
Special Education Teacher	Giselle Bachmeier	Giselle Bachmeier	1.22.
Regular Education Teacher	Anna Espinoza	A.Espinoza	1-22-
Student	Phoebe Delacroix	Phoebe	Jan 22_
Parent	Amy Delacroix	Amy Delacroix	1/22/
School Psychologist	Marty Goode	Martin F. Goode	Jan 22,

Rajesh Ansari

Rajesh is a seven-year-old second-grade student at Grendell Elementary School. Grendell is located in an upper-middle-class suburban neighborhood and enrolls 653 students in grades K–6 with 13% racial or ethnic minority and a few English learners. About 15% of the students receive special education services, slightly above average because the district houses two self-contained units for students with moderate to severe disabilities at the school. The most recent state-wide achievement testing results show that 55% of students are proficient in language arts, 59% in math, and 64% in science.

Family and Cultural Background

Ansari, Rajesh's father, and Mangai, his mother, are both professionals with advanced graduate degrees. Ansari earned a PhD in computer engineering and has an executive position in a fast-growing automotive technology company. Mangai has a PhD and is a professor of information science at a local university. Both parents were born in India and received their graduate degrees in America. Both are legal residents, and Rajesh is an American citizen.

Ansari and Mangai were born in Tamil Nadu and grew up in south India's information technology corridor. They attended respected undergraduate institutions and were well prepared for admission to graduate programs in the United States. Typical of many children raised in educated urban families, their parents spoke little of religion and never mentioned caste. Ansari and Mangai met in graduate school and were married in India with both families' consent. They are comfortably settled in their neighborhood and enjoy interacting with other young families. They encourage Rajesh to participate in activities of interest to him. Even though Ansari and Mangai are fluent in their native Tamil, they speak English at home to promote Rajesh's English fluency.

School Experience

This is Rajesh's second year at Grendell. He is considered a native English speaker and is acquiring academic English at a normal rate. At the end of his kindergarten year, his teacher, Ms. Castro, noted Rajesh's minimal progress recognizing and writing letters and simple words. She checked the school screening records and found that Rajesh's vision and hearing were in the normal range. She followed up at the beginning of the next school year and alerted Ms. Li, the first-grade teacher, about her concerns. Ms. Li monitored Rajesh's progress during the first two months of school while providing individual assistance with reading sounds and simple words. Rajesh's penmanship for letters and simple words seems to be progressing, but lack of improvement with reading convinced Ms. Li to confer with the special education team and to formally refer Rajesh for evaluation.

Ansari and Mangai were unfamiliar with special education and asked many questions about the law, the services available, and the process. Having their questions answered, they granted written permission to conduct the evaluation. The special education team leader assigned team members to conduct the assessments. Cognitive assessment indicated intellectual aptitude in the high average range. Achievement testing revealed significant deficits in segmenting and blending words orally and reading one-syllable words. Rajesh struggles to recognize letters and letter combinations and read them as sounds. The team met with his parents to explain the assessment results indicating Rajesh has specific learning disabilities, and after asking more clarifying questions the parents gave permission to hold an IEP meeting.

Individualized Education Program

1. Student Information

Student: _Rajesh Ansari_   3-yr Re-evaluation _10/21/_   Date of Birth _8/05/_

School _Grendell Elementary_   IEP Meeting _10/21/_   Classification _Specific learning disabilities_

IEP Due _10/20/_   Grade _2_   Initial Eligibility _10/21/_

2. Present Levels of Academic Achievement and Functional Performance

Reading

Woodcock-Johnson IV Tests of Cognitive Abilities© given 1/21/__ indicate Rajesh functions in the normal range of cognitive abilities. Woodcock-Johnson IV Tests of Achievement© (1/22/__) show that Rajesh can say the alphabet by rote. He cannot count, pronounce, blend, or segment syllables in spoken words. He does not associate long and short vowel sounds with common spellings or read common high frequency words by sight at the first-grade level. To progress in the Grade 2 curriculum, Rajesh needs to know and apply grade-level phonics and word analysis skills in decoding words (CCSS.ELA-Literacy.RF2.3) and read with sufficient accuracy and fluency to support comprehension (CCSS.ELA-Literacy.RF2.4).

3. Measurable Annual Goals

Reading

1. *Given second-grade one- and two-syllable regularly and irregularly spelled words and weekly opportunities to practice, Rajesh will read the words correctly with at least 95% accuracy, as measured by teacher observation records (CCSS.ELA-LITERACY.RF2.3).*

2. *Given passages at first-grade level from literature and weekly opportunities to practice, Rajesh will read at least 72 words correct per minute and answer such questions as who, what, where, when, why, and how to demonstrate understanding of key details in a text (CCSS.ELA-LITERACY.RL2.1) with 90% accuracy as measured by progress monitoring.*

3. *Given passages at second-grade level from literature and weekly opportunities to practice, Rajesh will use information gained from words in a print or digital text to tell the characters, setting, or plot (CCSS.ELA-LITERACY.RL2.7) with 90% accuracy as measured by teacher observation records.*

4. The IEP Team considered the following special factors

Behavior	Not needed.
Language	Not needed.
Braille	Not needed.
Communication	Not needed.
Assistive Technology	Not needed.

5. Special Education and Related Services needed to progress in the general curriculum

Special Education Service	Location	Time/Frequency	Related Service
Specially designed instruction for reading	Special education class	45 min 5x weekly	None

Program modifications, supports for school personnel, and/or supplementary aids in the regular education program

None

6. Participation in State & District Assessment

Participation Codes

S	Standard administration	No accommodations or modifications
A	Participate with accommodations	Does not invalidate, alter, or lower standard
M	Participate with modifications	Invalidates, alters, or lowers standard
AA	Participate using alternate assessment: ☐ Out-of-level CRT ☐ State alternate assessment	Aligned more closely with alternate curriculum than regular curriculum

		Criterion Referenced Tests (CRT)				State High School Competency Test			
	Accommodations	Lang Arts	Math	Science	Directed Writing Assessment	Reading	Writing	Math	Iowa Test of Basic Skills
Presentation	1. Direction read aloud in English	A	A	A					
	2. Questions read aloud in English		A	A		No			
	3. Directions signed								
	4. Questions signed					No			
	5. Screen reader					No			No
	6. Directions—oral translation								No
	7. Questions—oral translation	No			No	No	No		No
	8. Large print								
	9. Magnification devices								
	10. Braille								
	11. Tactile graphics								
	12. Audio amplification devices								
	13. Visual cues								
	14. Talking materials								
	15. Bilingual word lists	—	—	—	—				No
	16. Translated formulas	—		—	—	—	—		No
Response	17. Word processor—no spell check		—	—				—	—
	18. Calculation devices	—			—	—	—		No
	19. Write in test booklet								
	20. Scribe								
	21. Visual organizers								
	22. Graphic organizers								
	23. Speech-to-text conversion								No
	24. Brailler								
	25. Recording device								

	Accommodations	Criterion Referenced Tests (CRT)			Directed Writing Assessment	State High School Competency Test			Iowa Test of Basic Skills
		Lang Arts	Math	Science		Reading	Writing	Math	
Setting	26. Reduce distractions to student								
	27. Reduce distractions to others								
	28. Physical access—ADA								
Timing	29. Extended time								
	30. Multiple breaks								
	31. Schedule change								
Other	32. Other: Temporary (504 only)								

No: Accommodations not allowed   —: Not applicable

7. Regular Curriculum, Extracurricular, and Non-Academic Activities

The student will participate in the regular class, extracurricular, and other nonacademic activities except as noted in special education and related services or listed here:

8. Schedule for Written IEP Progress Reports to Parents

	Weekly	Biweekly	Monthly	Quarterly	Semiannually
Home note					
Progress report				X	
Parent conference					X
Report card	███████████████			X	███████████
Other					

9. Transition Plan (IEP beginning the year the student turns 16, or before if applicable)

Not applicable

10. Special Requirements for Graduation

Not applicable

11. Notices

Extended School Year: Extended school year (ESY) services are provided when the team determines the student requires special education and related services beyond the normal school year.

☐ Student is eligible for ESY

☒ Student is not eligible for ESY

Placement Review

☒ Initial placement ☐ Continue placement ☐ Change placement

IEP Team Participants

Position	Signature	Date
Parent	Ansari Nagaraj	10-21-
LEA Representative	Melba Stovall	10/21/
Special Education Teacher	Jackson Cave	Oct. 21,
General Education Teacher	Jenny Li	10/21/

Cadence Green

Cadence Green is a nine-year-old African American girl educationally classified as having an intellectual disability.

Family and Cultural Background

Cadence lives at home with her 13-year-old twin sisters, mom and dad, and maternal grandmother. Mr. Green works as a social media marketing director, and Mrs. Green works part-time as a private tennis coach. Their heritage is African American and the family has strong family and religious traditions. Cadence has been readily accepted by her neighbors and church congregation, who are actively engaged in integrating Cadence into the community. During one of Mrs. Green's prenatal screenings, her blood test suggested markers for an increased likelihood of her fetus having Down syndrome. Later tests confirmed this diagnosis and the parents were referred to the local Down syndrome association, who provided resources and referrals to the Greens. The family began attending support groups and trainings and the twins enrolled in the early intervention center's sibling workshops. Cadence received home-based services from the center until she was two years old; she then also began receiving center-based interventions. After a year of recurrent middle ear infections, at age 4 Cadence had tubes surgically placed into her eardrum, which significantly reduced the fluid in her ears and reduced the risk of future ear infections and hearing loss.

Prior School Experience

When Cadence turned three years old, her parents enrolled her in their neighborhood school, Brighton Heights Academy, a publicly funded charter school. She attended preschool alongside 10 other students, six of whom did not have disabilities. Cadence thrived in this environment and particularly enjoyed music and art. She learned to communicate using sign language, speech, and an augmentative communication device, and she received speech, physical, and occupational therapy along with specialized instruction. The multidisciplinary team classified her as having developmental delays.

At age 5, Cadence transitioned to a kindergarten class within Brighton Heights and received services according to her IEP. When she turned seven years old, the multidisciplinary team conducted a re-evaluation and determined that she has moderate intellectual disabilities. She spent her time during first to third grades in both general and special education classrooms. Her twin sisters regularly served as cross-age peer tutors in Cadence's classroom.

Current Schooling

Cadence is beginning the fourth grade at Brighton Heights Academy, which has 545 students with one principal and 25 teachers. The current fourth grade at Brighton consists of 76 students. Of these students, 63% (48) are white; 18% (14) are African American; 13% (10) are Asian/Pacific Islander; 5% (4) are Hispanic; 4% (3) have limited English proficiency; and 13% (10) have disabilities. Almost one-tenth (9%) of the students in the school are eligible for free/reduced lunch.

Cadence's fourth-grade teacher, Ms. Bower, is a veteran educator of 20 years and has a class of 25 students, three of whom have IEPs and receive special education services, including Cadence. Parents of children with special needs often request to have their children placed in Ms. Bower's class due to her reputation as a nurturing teacher who promotes inclusion and sets high expectations. Ms. Bower works closely with Mr. Keister, the special educator, to provide the special education services specified on Cadence's IEP. Ms. Bower is assisted by one part-time paraeducator to help all students in the class who need additional assistance, and the paraeducator provides frequent individual support to Cadence during math, English/Language Arts, P.E, and specialty classes (e.g., music, art). Cadence receives speech services from the licensed speech language pathologist at the school, who coordinates the integration of services into her school day and provides direct services to Cadence. Preferring speech to other modes of communication, Cadence receives therapy to enhance her speech production rather than sign language or using an electronic communication device.

Ms. Bower reports that Cadence is expected to engage in the same curricular activities as the other fourth-grade students, but she needs additional instruction and support in reading text materials, understanding abstract concepts, and staying on task. Cadence learns best when she is given additional time to complete tasks, tangible and pictorial materials, and short breaks.

Individualized Education Program

Student: _Cadence Green_   Birth date: _Sept. 12_   Grade: _4th_

IEP Date: _Sept. 19_   School: _Brighton Heights Academy_   Classification: _Intellectual Disability_

Present Levels of Academic Achievement and Functional Performance

MATH: According to results from the Woodcock-Johnson Tests of Achievement (Sept. 7–10), Cadence's math skills are at a first-grade level (e.g., she can accurately identify numbers 1–100, count objects to 10, identify four basic shapes). She cannot perform many of the prerequisite skills necessary to achieve the second-grade standards. To progress in the general education curriculum, Cadence needs to tell and write time from analog and digital clocks to the nearest five minutes (CCSS.Math.Content.2.MD.C.7), use addition/subtraction within 20 (CCSS.Math.Content.2.OA.B.2), and solve word problems involving bills and coins (CCSS.Math.Content.2.MD.C.8).

ENGLISH LANGUAGE ARTS: According to the Woodcock-Johnson Tests of Achievement (Sept. 7–10), Cadence's reading skills are at a first-grade level and she has strengths in visual processing, particularly with reading whole words. She has a basic command of the conventions of standard English grammar and usage when speaking and writing (e.g., writes brief narratives about sequenced events, uses verbs to convey a sense of past, present, and future; uses conjunctions). However, she is not currently performing the prerequisite skills required to meet second-grade standards. To progress in the general curriculum, she needs to use phonics and word recognition skills fluently at a second-grade level (CCSS.ELA-Literacy-RF.2.3 & CCSS.ELA-Literacy-RF.2.4); use print and digital dictionaries to determine meaning of words (CCSS.ELA-Literacy.L.2.2.E); and write elaborate narratives to describe actions, thoughts, and feelings (CCSS.ELA-Literacy.W.2.3).

COMMUNICATION: According to recent testing by the school audiologist (May 22), Cadence's hearing is within normal limits. Testing by the school speech-language pathologist (Sept. 4–6) indicates her receptive language is stronger than her expressive language; she has particular challenges with phonology, vocabulary, and syntax. Cadence can communicate using approximately 500 spoken words, which she uses in 3–5 word phrases/sentences, and is intelligible approximately 50% of the time. She struggles to participates in collaborative conversations with diverse partners (CCSS.ELA-Literacy-SL.2.1) because she interrupts others, and changes topics prematurely because she is not focusing on the conversation. To progress in the general curriculum Cadence needs to increase her skills in articulation, receptive/expressive vocabulary, syntax, and conversing with others.

FUNCTIONAL LIFE SKILLS: According to end-of-year data from her special educator and her parents, Cadence can moisturize her hair independently; she wants to brush her hair independently to remove tangles, but currently needs physical and verbal prompting for each step of this task.

Measurable Annual Goals

1. MATH: *When assessed on the State Alternate Assessment at the end of the school year, Cadence will increase her math skills to a 1.6 grade level in at least 80% of the tested sub-domains (EE.2.MD.7; EE.1.OAA.1; EE.2.MD.8)*

Benchmarks/Short-Term Objectives

a. *When given a clock, Cadence will tell and write the time to the nearest five minutes, including a.m. and p.m., with at least 80% accuracy, with at least two different types of clocks (digital and analog), and maintain the skill when probed weekly for two weeks.*

b. *When given addition and subtraction problems within 20, Cadence will solve the problems with at least 80% accuracy, in two different settings (general and special education classrooms) and maintain this skill when probed weekly for two weeks.*

c. *When given simple word problems involving dollar bills, quarters, dimes, nickels, and pennies, Cadence will use $ and ¢ symbols with at least 80% accuracy, with various types of word problems, and she will maintain this skill when probed weekly for two weeks.*

Student's progress toward goal measured by:

☐ formal assessment   ☐ criterion-referenced   ☒ curriculum-based   ☒ checklists
☐ work samples   ☐ self-monitor

2. **ENGLISH LANGUAGE ARTS:** *When assessed on the State Alternate Assessment at the end of the school year, Cadence will increase her reading and writing skills to a 1.6 grade level in at least 80% of the tested sub-domains (EE.RF.2.3; EE.R1.2.4; EE.W.2.6).*

Benchmarks/Short-Term Objectives

a. *When given various second-grade reading passages, Cadence will read each passage fluently with at least 90% accuracy and maintain this skill when probed weekly for four weeks.*

b. *When reading a second-grade reading passage that contains words she does not understand, Cadence will use a digital dictionary (or ask Siri/Google/Alexa) to find each word, read (or listen to) the definition, and explain to a peer or adult the meaning of each word, with at least 80% accuracy, and she will maintain this skill when probed weekly for two weeks.*

c. *After having been read/told a story, or having watched a video, Cadence will write a narrative that recounts the events, including details that describe actions, thoughts, and feelings, with at least 80% accuracy, and she will maintain this skill when probed weekly for at two weeks.*

Student's progress toward goal measured by:

☐ formal assessment   ☒ criterion-referenced   ☒ curriculum-based   ☐ checklists
☒ work samples   ☐ self-monitor

3. **COMMUNICATION:** *Cadence will increase her speech intelligibility, to at least 80% of observed occurrences, with at least three different people in at least three different settings, while using appropriate vocabulary, syntax, and turn-taking. She will maintain these skills when probed weekly for two weeks (EE.SL.2.1).*

Benchmarks/Short-Term Objectives

a. *When Cadence is engaged in a conversation with a peer, her speech will be intelligible at least 80% of observed occurrences, and she will use appropriate vocabulary, syntax, vocabulary, and turn-taking with at least three different people in three different settings, and she will maintain this skill when probed weekly for two weeks.*

b. *When Cadence is engaged in a conversation with a peer, her speech will be intelligible at least 70% of observed occurrences, and she will use appropriate vocabulary, syntax, and turn-taking with at least three different people in three different settings, and she will maintain this skill when probed weekly for two weeks.*

c. *When Cadence is engaged in a conversation with a peer, her speech will be intelligible at least 60% of observed occurrences, and she will use appropriate vocabulary, syntax, and turn-taking with at least three different people in three different settings, and she will maintain this skill when probed weekly for two weeks.*

Student's progress toward goal measured by:

☐ formal assessment   ☐ criterion-referenced   ☐ curriculum-based   ☒ checklists
☐ work samples   ☐ self-monitor

4. FUNCTIONAL LIFE SKILLS: *When Cadence needs to brush her hair, she will complete all tasks within the task analysis within five minutes with no prompts, using various brushes, picks, combs, 4/5 times weekly. She will maintain this skill when probed weekly for two consecutive weeks.*

Benchmarks/Short-Term Objectives

a. *When Cadence is asked to brush her hair, she will correctly* find her brush *within one minute, 4/5 times without prompting, using various hair instruments, and she will maintain this skill when probed weekly for two consecutive weeks.*

b. *When Cadence is asked to brush her hair, she will correctly find her brush, and use it to* detangle the left side *of her hair within two minutes, 4/5 times without prompting, using various hair instruments, and she will maintain this skill when probed weekly for two consecutive weeks.*

c. *When Cadence is asked to brush her hair, she will correctly find her brush, and use it to detangle the left side of her hair and the* right side *within three minutes, 4/5 times without prompting, using various hair instruments, and she will maintain this skill when probed weekly for two consecutive weeks.*

d. *When Cadence is asked to brush her hair, she will correctly find her brush, and use it to detangle the left and right side of her hair, and the* back *within four minutes, 4/5 times without prompting, using various hair instruments, and she will maintain this skill when probed weekly for two consecutive weeks.*

e. *When Cadence* notices her hair needs to be brushed, *she will correctly find her brush and use it to detangle the left, right, and back sides of her hair within five minutes, 4/5 times without prompting, using various hair instruments, and she will maintain this skill when probed weekly for two consecutive weeks.*

Student's progress toward goal measured by:

☐ formal assessment   ☐ criterion-referenced   ☐ curriculum-based   ☒ checklists
☐ work samples   ☐ self-monitor

Special Education Services to Achieve Annual Goals and Advance in General Curriculum

R = Regular class   S = Special class   O = Other   D = Daily   W = Weekly   M = Monthly

Service	Location	Time	Frequency	Begin date	Duration
Specially designed instruction	R S O	*5 hrs*	D W M	*9/20*	1 yr
Specially designed instruction	R S O	*1 hrs*	D W M	*9/20*	1 yr

Related Services to Benefit from Special Education

Service	Location	Time	Frequency	Begin date	Duration
Speech-language services	R S O: *Speech Therapy Room*	*20 min*	D W M	*9/20*	1 yr

Program Modifications and/or Supplementary Aids and Services in Regular Classes

Modifications/Personnel Support	Frequency	Supplementary Aids and Services	Frequency
Support training and consultation for teacher and paraeducators	D W <u>M</u>	*Paraeducator in general classroom 4 hrs.*	<u>D</u> W M

Applicable Special Factors

Factor	Not Needed	In IEP
Positive behavior instruction and support when behavior impedes learning of student or others	✔	
Language needs for student with limited English proficiency	✔	
Braille instruction for student who is blind or visually impaired	✔	
Communication and/or language services for student who is deaf or hard of hearing or has other communication needs		✔
Assistive technology devices or services	✔	

Participation in Regular Class, Extracurricular, and Nonacademic Activities

The student will participate in the regular class, extracurricular, and other nonacademic activities except as noted in special education and related services or listed here: *Cadence will not participate in math and language arts in the general education classroom 1–2 times per week so she can receive 1:1 instruction from the special education teacher.*

Schedule for Written IEP Progress Reports to Parents

	Weekly	Biweekly	Monthly	Quarterly	Semiannually
Home note	X				
Progress report			X		
Parent conference					X
Report card				X	
Other					

Transition Plan

Complete and attach for students age 16 and older.

N/A

Participation in State and District Assessments

Participation Codes

S	Standard administration	No accommodations or modifications
A	Participate with accommodations	Does not invalidate, alter, or lower standard
M	Participate with modifications	Invalidates, alters, or lowers standard
AA	Participate using alternate assessment: ☐ Out-of-level CRT ☒ State alternate assessment	Aligned more closely with alternate curriculum than general education curriculum

State and District Assessment Matrix

Enter appropriate participation code for each applicable assessment.

Grade	Kindergarten Pretest	Kindergarten Posttest	State Criterion Referenced Math	State Criterion Referenced Language Arts	State Criterion Referenced Science	Iowa Test of Basic Skills	National Assessment Educational Progress
K							
1							
2							
3							
4			AA	AA	AA	AA	AA
5							
6							
7							
8							
9							
10							
11							
12							

Accommodations and Modifications

List specific accommodations and modifications for assessments.

Not applicable. Cadence's performance is evaluated using the state alternate assessment.

Alternate Assessment

State why student cannot participate in regular assessment.

Cadence's skills in math and language arts are approximately two years behind her typically developing peers; her poor communication skills and limited attention span impair her ability to successfully demonstrate achievement on standardized tests.

State why selected alternate assessment is appropriate.

Cadence was administered the State Alternate Assessment at the beginning of this year and was able to demonstrate her skills, given multiple testing breaks, prompts to stay on task, concrete examples, and multiple explanations of the tasks, in a 1:1 setting.

Special Requirements for Graduation

Not applicable

Extended School Year

Extended school year (ESY) services are provided when the team determines the student requires special education and related services beyond the normal school year.

☒ Student is eligible for ESY

☐ Student is not eligible for ESY

Placement Review

☐ Initial placement ☒ Continue placement ☐ Change placement

IEP Team Participants

Jeanna Green	Parent
Lewis Green	Parent
Shantelle Hancock	LEA Representative
MaryAnn Bower	Regular Class Teacher
Sam Kiester	Special Education Teacher
Lane Graham	School Psychologist
Jaynie Hallam	Speech-Language Pathologist

If parent signature is missing, provide a copy of the IEP and Procedural Safeguards and check below:

☐ Did not attend (document efforts to involve parent)

☐ Via telephone

☐ Other _____

Comments

Keej Moua

Keej Moua is a 19-year-old Hmong-American young man who is educationally classified as having autism.

Family and Cultural Background

Keej lives at home with his mother and two younger siblings. He has four older siblings who no longer live at home. Keej's parents divorced when he was four years old and Keej visits his father monthly. Mrs. Moua has worked full time in a candy factory for the past 20 years. Having immigrated from Laos to the United States as children, both of Keej's parents speak English, but Mrs. Moua is more comfortable speaking Hmong, Thai, or Lao. Both parents prefer to speak Hmong when with their children. Although Keej has limited communication skills, when he does speak, it is in English, and his family reports that he seems to understand many basic phrases in Hmong.

Mrs. Moua has assumed the role of the primary contact person for the school. She has been very appreciative of the education provided to Keej, and she has shown her respect to school personnel by agreeing to all of their educational recommendations. She is not concerned about Keej achieving independence, as she and her other children feel familial obligation, devotion, and loyalty for taking care of him for the rest of his life. However, Keej's siblings wonder if he will ever be able to travel independently, make friends, or enjoy leisure time outside of the home.

When Keej began having seizures at age 13, his mother was reluctant to have him treated by a medical doctor, preferring their traditional approach based on shamanism. With the assistance of a Hmong family advocate/cultural broker, Keej's seizures are now treated with an eclectic, culturally sensitive approach that has diminished his seizures to approximately one every six months.

Prior School Experience

When he was three years old, Keej's parents noticed he was not speaking as well as his older siblings had at that age. They also noticed unusual mannerisms, such as lining up his toys, being peculiar with what he would eat, and feeling irritated with certain pieces of clothing. They weren't sure how to handle his frequent tantrums but kept their concerns to themselves. When he was still not talking at age 4, a concerned neighbor/family advocate accompanied Mrs. Moua to a community preschool program that served children with developmental delays. There Keej was evaluated and determined eligible to receive special education services from the local school district under the classification of Developmental Delay. The staff referred the Mouas to a pediatric psychologist for a full evaluation that could trigger appropriate intensive services, but the family declined, somewhat leery of Western medical practices.

The school district provided Keej with behavioral, developmental, communication, and physical therapy services five days a week for 2 ½ hours a day in an integrated preschool classroom. Keej also received applied behavior analysis therapy at home twice per week. At age 5 he began attending kindergarten at his neighborhood school in a program solely for children with developmental delays. At age 7, the school's multidisciplinary team evaluated and classified Keej as having autism. Later that year, the family advocate accompanied the Mouas to visit a pediatric psychologist, and Keej was subsequently diagnosed with autism spectrum disorder. The family then qualified for insurance coverage for outside services at an autism center, but they were unable to obtain transportation to the center, and therefore, Keej received only school-based services.

Beginning in first grade and throughout his grade school education, Keej was taught alongside his typically developing peers and was provided in-class support by special educators, behavior specialists, speech language pathologists with expertise in augmentative and alternative communication, and paraeducators, in accordance with his IEP. Because of his regular meltdowns and lack of progress in the general curriculum during his first-grade year, he began receiving pull-out services for reading, math, behavioral/social-emotional services, and speech-language services. In junior high school, Keej continued to receive special education services in a classroom for students with disabilities, while still taking 1–2 general education classes each quarter. In high school he continued to take a few general education classes, but also began taking classes in the transition program, where he engaged in career exploration and learned many essential work skills.

Current Schooling

After his high school senior year, Keej enrolled in a district-sponsored college program for students with developmental disabilities, coordinated by Mr. Allred, a District 5 special educator and transition specialist. Keej is working to earn his certificate of completion from high school rather than a diploma. The curriculum in the district's Lifelong Success Transition Program housed on the campus of St. Joseph's Community College is tailored to meet 18–21 year-old students' needs according to their IEPs and Post-Secondary Transition Plans. It provides opportunities for students to take classes with their same-age peers, complete apprenticeships, participate in social and recreational activities, and hold jobs on campus or in the community. The program is housed at the St. Joseph's, and enrolls 30 students aged 18–21. Of these students, 12 (40%) are white; 7 (23%) are Asian; 5 (17%) are Hispanic; 4 (13%) are African American, and 2 (7%) are from other ethnic/racial categories. Also, 5 (17%) have limited English proficiency.

Keej is currently auditing a Veterinary Tech class and accompanying lab and a photography class on campus with other college students, including a peer mentor, who is enrolled in these classes for course credit and a grade. Keej is enrolled in math, reading, daily life skills, and employability classes with other students who have developmental disabilities. He works alongside typically developing peers for one hour a day in the library where he sorts and stacks books and is paid a competitive wage. Another library student employee is his job coach, supported by funds from Vocational Rehabilitation. Keej especially enjoys his photography class, Vet Tech lab, and his employment at the college library.

Individualized Education Program

Student: _Keej Moua_   Birth date: _February 15_   IEP Date: _February 20_

School: _St. Joseph Community College (District 5's Lifelong Success Transition Program)_

Grade: _12+_   Classification: _Autism_

Present Levels of Academic Achievement and Functional Performance

Preschool students: Describe how the disability affects the student's participation in appropriate activities.

School-age students: Describe how the disability affects the student's involvement and progress in the general curriculum.

MATH: Informal assessment (January 12–16) indicates that Keej can use Excel Spreadsheets to enter data into rows and columns, but he can use the "function" feature for addition, subtraction, multiplication, and division with only 45% accuracy, a skill that is required for a vet tech to prepare invoices and record inventory. He measures volume using standard units of measurement with 50% accuracy, a skill that is necessary for disinfecting instruments, preparing cleaning solutions, and completing other related tasks in the vet tech lab. Keej uses Venmo, PayPal, and his bank debit card to make monetary transactions; however, he misplaces the decimal point approximately 55% of the time, resulting in inaccurate, and sometimes costly, transactions.

Although he has interest and emerging proficiency in these areas, his levels of accuracy and independence in these areas of math affect his ability to reach his post-secondary goals. Keej needs to solve real-world problems involving addition and subtraction of decimals (EE.N-CN.2.b [Essential Elements alternate curriculum]), measure liquid volumes using standard units (EE.4.MD.2.b), and make monetary transactions including decimals (EE.N-CN.2.b) with at least 80% accuracy.

LANGUAGE ARTS: Based upon informal passage fluency measures (January 19–20), Keej has mastered English reading standards to a 4.5 grade level, reading 60 words correct per minute, but cannot use accuracy, fluency, or comprehension skills to read books of his choice because they are typically written at a 5.5 grade level or higher. Based upon classroom observations and skill checklists (January 20–21), Keej can transcribe handwritten notes 60% accuracy, a skill that is used daily in the vet tech lab, as he inputs the veterinarian's lab notes into the computer. He has mastered writing composition to the 3.0 grade level but cannot use a spellchecker with more than 50% accuracy to check his work (he has difficulty choosing the right spelling for each word he is checking).

In order to reach his post-secondary goals, Keej needs to read text comprised of familiar words with accuracy and understanding at the 5.5 grade level, use context to confirm or self-correct word recognition when reading (EE.RF.5.4); and write to share information supported by details and with correct spelling (EE.W.5.2).

SOCIAL/EMOTIONAL: Keej has a positive demeanor but gets anxious about 80% of the time when his environments are loud, routines are disrupted, his schedule changes, and when asked to engage in new activities. When he is bored, he often engages in self-stimulatory behavior such as rocking and hand flapping. When anxious, he tends to pace around the room and recite lines from his favorite Disney movies. Although he doesn't get angry often, when he does, he hits the left side of his head with his fist. When he is angry, he typically does not speak but makes loud noises to show his emotions.

While Keej is generally pleasant, his outbursts are upsetting to him and to others, restricting his ability to meet his post-secondary goals. He needs to learn how to control his behaviors when he is feeling anxious, angry, or otherwise upset. Keej currently has a Behavior Intervention Plan based upon the Functional Behavior Assessment conducted by the Behavior Consultant last April, which will need to be re-examined.

COMMUNICATION: Keej speaks and understands English and he understands some Hmong; however, he does not have a wide range of pragmatic language in either language. Based upon the speech-language pathologist's assessment (January 22–23), Keej articulates clearly and regularly uses approximately 400 words in simple 1–5 word phrases. He uses both immediate and delayed echolalia, primarily to talk about his favorite movies and animals, but currently he cannot initiate conversation on other topics without prompting. He uses an augmentative communication app on a smartphone to engage in brief conversations.

In order to meet his post-secondary goals to participate more fully in social relationships and his community, Keej needs to increase his pragmatic language usage in both English and Hmong, and initiate and sustain conversation on a wider range of topics with more complexity in vocabulary and sentence length, with and without a communication device.

FUNCTIONAL LIFE SKILLS: Keej is interested in using the city's rental scooter program, but he does not know how to get from his home to the college without turn-by-turn verbal prompting.

In order to reach his post-secondary goals, Keej needs to increase his independence with accessing the scooter system so he can access places of interest independently or with a peer.

CAREER/VOCATIONAL: Keej participated in a job sampling program during high school and found that he enjoys working in environments where the social and communication demands are not high, and the work is routine. In his current work in the library, Keej is competent in shelving books. His peer mentor works alongside him and helps if necessary. In his vet tech lab, however, he is unable to complete the required tasks without verbal prompting.

To reach his current post-secondary goals and to prepare for a wider range of vocational opportunities, Keej needs to independently engage in a wider range of work tasks.

Postsecondary Transition Plan

Student _Keej Moua_   Birthdate _February 15_   Date _February 20_

School _Lifelong Success Transition Program at St. Joseph Community College_

Grade _12+_   Classification _Autism_

Check one:

☐ Graduate with a regular diploma. Expected Graduation Date: _N/A_

☒ Graduate with a certificate of completion. Expected Completion Date: _May 31_

Student's Strengths, Preferences, Interests, and Needs

Include a brief narrative based upon interviews, career assessments, and multiple observations over time.

> _Results from the Brigance Transition Skills Inventory, functional vocational evaluations, interviews, and observations from September through January indicate Keej loves small animals and enjoys attending his Veterinary Tech class and lab at St. Joseph Community College. He also enjoys the photography class held at the college. A peer mentor helps him as needed in these two classes. Sometimes when it gets too loud and confusing for Keej in these environments, his mentor takes him for short walks to help him calm down._
>
> _Keej thrives in his job at the library, where the environment is quiet, and his work is predictable. He has a Vocational Rehabilitation job coach who has taught Keej how to sort and shelve books. Keej's math skills are sufficient for this job, but he has only worked in one section of the library._
>
> _Keej is interested in keeping his job at the library and taking another class in the Veterinary Tech program._
>
> _Currently, Keej's older brother drives him to the college, but this brother is moving next year and will be unable to help in the future. Keej expressed some interest in riding a scooter to campus, and when given the opportunity to use a scooter, he enjoyed it but could not ride safely on his own. He is currently afraid to ride the city bus, so this option, among others, will be explored at a later date. Keej's mother is not concerned about his skill development in household duties, money management, and community involvement at this time._

Measurable Postsecondary Goals, Activities, and Services

Based upon the assessments regarding the student's strengths, preferences, and interests, list the goals the student wants to achieve after completion of high school/post-high school programs. Refer to IEP goals or explain how postsecondary activities/services will be provided. Indicate people, resources, and agencies that can help (e.g., colleges, employment agencies, transition specialists).

Postsecondary Education/Vocational Training

Postsecondary Goal: *After graduating with a Certificate of Completion, Keej will receive training in a local small animal clinic and public library.*

Supporting IEP Goal	Transition Activities/ Services	Person/Agency Responsible
#6—Career/Vocational	*While Keej currently works at the college's library, he only works in one section. An evaluation of the demands of working in other sections and Keej's skills will need to be conducted.*	*Vocational Rehabilitation*
#6—Career/Vocational	*Peer Mentor*	*St. Joseph Community College's Accessibility Center*
#6—Career/Vocational	*Transition services*	*District 5, partnering with St. Joseph Community College*
#1—Math #2—English/Language Arts #3—Social/Emotional #6—Career/Vocational	*Specialized instruction*	*District 5 Special Education Team*
#4—Communication	*Bilingual speech-language services*	*District 5 Speech Language Pathologist*

OR indicate why service is not needed:

☐ Student functions independently in educational/vocational settings.

☐ Other: _____

Employment

Postsecondary Goal: *After graduating with a Certificate of Completion, Keej will be employed at a small animal clinic and/or public library.*

Supporting IEP Goal	Transition Activities/Services	Person/Agency Responsible
	No employment transition services required until one year prior to Keej's 22nd birthday. See "Postsecondary Education/Vocational Training" for current training activities.	*Vocational Rehabilitation*

OR indicate why service is not needed:

☐ Student functions independently in work settings.

☐ Other: _____

Independent Living		
Postsecondary Goal: *After graduating with a Certificate of Completion, Keej will live at home and ride a scooter or the city bus (e.g., in the winter) to his place of training/employment.*		

Housing	Transportation
☐ Skilled Care Facility ☐ Group Home ☐ Supervised Apartment ☐ Supported Living ☒ Family home ☐ Apartment ☐ Home of own	☒ Independent transportation (e.g., walk, bicycle, car, scooter) ☒ Public transportation (e.g., bus, train) ☐ Specialized transportation ☐ Other:

Supporting IEP Goal	Transition Activities/ Services	Person/Agency Responsible
#1—Math *#5—Functional Life Skills*	*Electric scooter access card; bus card*	*District 5*
	Apply for state ID card	*District 5*

OR indicate why service is not needed:

☐ Student functions independently in home/community settings.

☐ Other: _____

Age of Majority

On or before the student's 17th birthday, inform the student and parent(s) of the rights under IDEA that will transfer to the student upon reaching the age of majority.

Date informed: *January 15 (Documents provided in Hmong & English language)*

Nonparticipation in Transition Planning

If the student did not participate in this plan, indicate the steps taken to ensure the student's preferences were considered.

Not Applicable

If a representative of an agency responsible for providing an activity did not participate, indicate the steps that will be taken to obtain the participation of the agency.

Not Applicable

Measurable Annual Goals

1. <u>MATH:</u> *When assessed at the end of the school year, Keej will increase his math skills to at least 80% accuracy in each of the following skill areas: compute three-digit addition, subtraction, multiplication, and division problems; measure volume using standard units of measurement; and use decimal points accurately with up to five-digit numerals.*

Benchmarks/Short-Term Objectives

a. *When given a functional math problem requiring four-digit addition, subtraction, multiplication, or division, Keej will find the sum/difference/ product/quotient with at least 80% accuracy, using the "function" feature in Excel, and he will maintain the skill when probed weekly for at least four weeks.*

b. *When given a written volume amount and beaker or other container, Keej will independently measure the specified amount with at least 90% accuracy over 10 consecutive trials, using various units of measurement (i.e., fluid ounces, cups, pints, quarts, and gallons), and he will maintain this skill when probed weekly for at least four weeks.*

c. *When engaging in a financial transaction, Keej will enter the required amount, including dollars and cents, with no more than two verbal/pictorial prompts per transaction, using at least two different platforms (e.g., Venmo, PayPal, debit card), and he will maintain this skill when probed weekly for at least four weeks.*

Student's progress toward goal measured by:

☒ Curriculum-Based Measures ☐ Behavior Observation ☒ Skills Checklist
☐ Work Sample ☐ Test Results ☐ Other

For students with post-secondary transition plans, indicate which goal domain(s) this annual goal will support:

☒ Post-Secondary Education/Vocational Training ☒ Employment ☒ Independent Living

2. <u>ENGLISH LANGUAGE ARTS:</u> *When assessed at the end of the school year, Keej will increase his reading, writing, and spelling skills with at least 80% accuracy, based upon alternate curriculum-based measures.*

Benchmarks/Short-Term Objectives

a. *When given a choice of books written in English on a 5.5 grade level, Keej will choose a book and independently read it with at least 70 words correct per minute, with at least three books on different topics, and he will maintain this skill when probed weekly for at least four weeks.*

b. *When given a legible handwritten note including words and numbers, Keej will transcribe each note into a computer software program with at least 80% accuracy over two consecutive weeks, using notes from at least two different people, and he will maintain this skill when probed weekly for at least four weeks.*

c. *When asked to write a passage about a relevant topic using a word processing program, Keej will write clear sentences using correct spelling with at least 80% accuracy over two consecutive weeks, with various topics, and he will maintain this skill when probed weekly for at least four weeks.*

Student's progress toward goal measured by:

☒ Curriculum-Based Measures ☐ Behavior Observation ☒ Skills Checklist
☐ Work Sample ☐ Test Results ☐ Other

For students with post-secondary transition plans, indicate which goal domain(s) this annual goal will support:

☒ Post-Secondary Education/Vocational Training ☒ Employment ☐ Independent Living

3. SOCIAL/EMOTIONAL: *When changes to the activities or expectations are made and when he is anxious, bored, or angry, Keej will use self-calming and distracting activities at least 50% of the time without displaying emotionally distressing behaviors.*

Benchmarks/Short-Term Objectives

a. *When the schedule, activities, or expectations change and when anxious, bored, or angry, Keej will engage in appropriate self-calming or distracting activities to reduce his anxiety over these changes at least 50% of the time over five consecutive school days, and he will maintain this skill when probed weekly for at least four weeks with at least four different types of activities.*

b. *When the schedule, activities, or expectations change and when anxious, bored, or angry, Keej will engage in appropriate self-calming or distracting activities to reduce his anxiety over these changes at least 75% of the time over five consecutive school days, and he will maintain this skill when probed weekly for at least four weeks with at least four different types of activities.*

Student's progress toward goal measured by:

☐ Curriculum-Based Measures ☒ Behavior Observation ☐ Skills Checklist
☐ Work Sample ☐ Test Results ☐ Other

For students with post-secondary transition plans, indicate which goal domain(s) this annual goal will support:

☒ Post-Secondary Education/Vocational Training ☒ Employment ☒ Independent Living

4. COMMUNICATION: *When in a social setting, Keej will increase his use of English and Hmong pragmatic language and initiate conversation with or without a communication device or app, using at least five-word novel sentences/phrases over at least 50% of observed occurrences, and he will maintain this skill when probed weekly for at least four weeks.*

Benchmarks/Short-Term Objectives

a. *When in a social setting with a bilingual communication partner who speaks Hmong and English, Keej will answer questions about himself (e.g., address, friends' names, hobbies) at least 50% of observed occurrences and maintain this skill when probed weekly for at least four weeks.*

b. *When in a setting without his communication device, Keej will initiate conversation with a peer, discussing a new topic at least 50% of observed occurrences and maintain this skill when probed weekly for at least four weeks, on at least five different topics.*

c. *When in a setting with his communication device, Keej will initiate conversation with a peer, discussing a new topic at least 50% of observed occurrences and maintain this skill when probed weekly for at least four weeks, on at least five different topics.*

Student's progress toward goal measured by:

☐ Curriculum-Based Measures   ☐ Behavior Observation   ☒ Skills Checklist
☐ Work Sample   ☐ Test Results   ☐ Other

For students with post-secondary transition plans, indicate which goal domain(s) this annual goal will support:

☒ Post-Secondary Education/Vocational Training   ☒ Employment   ☒ Independent Living

5. **FUNCTIONAL LIFE SKILLS:** *When accompanied by his peer mentor and given a digital map on a smartphone, Keej will independently use a city rental scooter to transport himself between home and college with 100% accuracy.*

Benchmarks/Short-Term Objectives

a. *By May, when accompanied by his peer mentor and given a digital map on a smartphone, Keej will independently use an electric scooter to transport himself from home to college, arriving safely and on time, with 100% accuracy, and he will maintain this skill when probed weekly for at least two months.*

b. *By October, when accompanied by his peer mentor and given a digital map on a smartphone, Keej will independently use an electric scooter to transport himself from college to home, arriving safely and on time, with 100% accuracy, and he will maintain this skill when probed weekly for at least two months.*

Student's progress toward goal measured by:

☐ Curriculum-Based Measures   ☐ Behavior Observation   ☒ Skills Checklist
☐ Work Sample   ☐ Test Results   ☐ Other

For students with post-secondary transition plans, indicate which goal domain(s) this annual goal will support:

☒ Post-Secondary Education/Vocational Training   ☒ Employment   ☒ Independent Living

6. **CAREER/VOCATIONAL:** *When working in the vet tech lab and given audio prompts, via a smartphone, Keej will independently complete a range of at least five various tasks (e.g., feeding, exercising, bathing, and monitoring animals; disinfecting cages) with at least 80% accuracy over three consecutive work days, and he will maintain these skills when probed weekly for at least four weeks.*

Benchmarks/Short-Term Objectives

a. *When given one work task to complete and picture/audio prompts describing each step in the task, Keej will complete the task independently with at least 80% accuracy, over three consecutive work days, and he will maintain this skill when probed weekly for at least four weeks.*

b. *When given one work task to complete and audio prompts describing each step in the task, Keej will complete the task independently with at least 80% accuracy, over three consecutive work days, and he will maintain this skill when probed weekly for at least four weeks.*

c. *When given one new work task to complete and no prompts, Keej will complete the task independently with at least 80% accuracy, over three consecutive workdays, and he will maintain this skill when probed weekly for at least four weeks.*

Student's progress toward goal measured by:

☐ Curriculum-Based Measures   ☐ Behavior Observation   ☒ Skills Checklist

☒ Work Sample   ☐ Test Results   ☐ Other

For students with post-secondary transition plans, indicate which goal domain(s) this annual goal will support:

☒ Post-Secondary Education/Vocational Training   ☒ Employment   ☒ Independent Living

Special Education Services to Achieve Annual Goals and Advance in General Curriculum

R = Regular class   S = Special class   O = Other   D = Daily   W = Weekly   M = Monthly

Service	Provider	Location	Time Frequency	Begin date	Duration
Specially designed instruction	*District 5 Special Educators and Paraeducators*	R S <u>O</u>: *St. Joseph's Community College*	*20 hrs.* D <u>W</u> M	*2/21*	*1 yr.*

Related Services to Benefit from Special Education

Service	Provider	Location	Time	Frequency	Begin date	Duration
Speech-language services (English & Hmong)	*District 5 Bilingual Speech-Language Pathologist*	*R S <u>O</u>: St. Joseph's Community College*	*60 min.*	D <u>W</u> M	*2/21*	*1 yr.*
Behavioral services & consultation	*District 5 Behavioral Specialist*	*R S <u>O</u>: St. Joseph's Community College*	*30 min.*	D <u>W</u> M	*2/21*	*1 yr.*
Social skills group	*District 5 School Psychologist*	*R S <u>O</u>: St. Joseph's Community College*	*60 min.*	D <u>W</u> M	*2/21*	*1 yr.*
Transportation	*District 5 Paraeducator*	*R S <u>O</u>: Community*	*Appx. 30 min.*	<u>D</u> W M	*2/21*	*1 yr.*

Program Modifications and/or Supplementary Aids and Services in Regular Classes

Modifications/Personnel Support	Frequency	Supplementary Aids and Services	Frequency
Training for peer mentor	D W <u>M</u>	*Visual support systems*	<u>D</u> W M

Applicable Special Factors

Factor	Not Needed	In IEP
Positive behavior instruction and support when behavior impedes learning of student or others		✔
Language needs for student with limited English proficiency		✔
Braille instruction for student who is blind or visually impaired	✔	
Communication and/or language services for student who is deaf or hard of hearing or has other communication needs		✔
Assistive technology devices or services		✔

Participation in Regular Class, Extracurricular, and Nonacademic Activities

The student will participate in the regular class, extracurricular, and other nonacademic activities except as noted in special education and related services or listed here:

Keej is a post-high school student and will participate in elective classes (audit, not for a grade) with his typically developing peers at the community college except for when he is receiving small group or individualized services (e.g., speech therapy).

Schedule for Written IEP Progress Reports to Parents

	Weekly	Biweekly	Monthly	Quarterly	Semiannually
Home note	✔				
Progress report		✔			
Parent conference					✔
Report card				✔	
Other					

Post-Secondary Transition Plan

Complete and attach for students age 16 and older. *See Attached.*

Participation in State and District Assessments

Participation Codes

S	Standard administration	No accommodations or modifications
A	Participate with accommodations	Does not invalidate, alter, or lower standard
M	Participate with modifications	Invalidates, alters, or lowers standard
AA	Participate using alternate assessment: ☐ Out-of-level Criterion Referenced Test ☐ State alternate assessment	Aligned more closely with alternate curriculum than general education curriculum

State and District Assessment Matrix

Enter appropriate participation code for each applicable assessment.

Not applicable for Keej, as he is a post-high school student.

Accommodations	Criterion Referenced Tests (CRT)			Directed Writing Assessment	State High School Competency Test			Iowa Test of Basic Skills
	Lang Arts	Math	Science		Reading	Writing	Math	
1. Direction read aloud in English								
2. Questions read aloud in English					No			
3. Directions signed								
4. Questions signed					No			
5. Screen reader					No			No
6. Directions—oral translation								No
7. Questions—oral translation	No			No	No	No		No
8. Large print								
9. Magnification devices								
10. Braille								
11. Tactile graphics								
12. Audio amplification devices								
13. Visual cues								
14. Talking materials								
15. Bilingual word lists	—	—	—	—				No
16. Translated formulas	—		—	—	—	—		No

(Presentation)

| | Criterion Referenced Tests (CRT) | | | Directed Writing Assessment | State High School Competency Test | | | Iowa Test of Basic Skills |
Accommodations	Lang Arts	Math	Science	Directed Writing Assessment	Reading	Writing	Math	Iowa Test of Basic Skills
Response 17. Word processor—no spell check		—	—				—	—
18. Calculation devices	—			—	—	—		No
19. Write in test booklet								
20. Scribe								
21. Visual organizers								
22. Graphic organizers								
23. Speech-to-text conversion								No
24. Brailler								
25. Recording device								
Setting 26. Reduce distractions to student								
27. Reduce distractions to others								
28. Physical access—ADA								
Timing 29. Extended time								
30. Multiple breaks								
31. Schedule change								
Other 32. Other: Temporary (504 only)								

No: Accommodations not allowed —: Not applicable

Accommodations and Modifications

List specific accommodations and modifications for assessments.

None. Because Keej is auditing his community college courses, he is not required to complete the course assessments.

Alternate Assessment

State why student cannot participate in regular assessment.

Regular assessment is not required for Keej's typically developing peers (age 19); therefore, he will not participate in state or district-wide assessments.

State why selected alternate assessment is appropriate.

Because Keej is 19 years old and being served in a post-secondary transition program, curriculum-based, transition, and community-based alternate assessments are used to derive appropriate instructional goals.

Extended School Year

Extended school year (ESY) services are provided when the team determines the student will not benefit if services are not provided during the normal summer break.

☐ Student is eligible for ESY

☒ Student is not eligible for ESY

Placement Review

Consider the least restrictive environment in which the student will be educated to the maximum extent appropriate with students who do not have disabilities.

☐ Initial placement   ☒ Continue placement   ☐ Change placement

Placement Continuum (Pre-K)	Placement Continuum (K–12)	Placement Continuum (Post-Secondary)
☐ Early childhood setting ☐ Early childhood special education ☐ Home ☐ Part-time early childhood/part-time early childhood special education ☐ Public separate school ☐ Private separate school ☐ Public residential facility ☐ Private residential facility ☐ Homebound/hospital	☐ Regular class at least 80% of time ☐ Regular class 40–70% of time ☐ Regular class less than 40% of time ☐ Public separate school ☐ Private separate school ☐ Public residential facility ☐ Private residential facility ☐ Homebound/hospital	☐ Separate classes/ program in high school ☐ Off-campus transition program ☒ Transition program on college campus ☐ Public separate school ☐ Private separate school ☐ Public residential facility ☐ Private residential facility ☐ Homebound/hospital

The team determined the student's least restrictive environment:

☐ Initial placement   ☒ Continue placement   ☐ Change placement

IEP Team Participants

Mai Yer Moua	Parent
Keej Moua	Student
Winn Allred	Special Educator, Lifelong Success Transition Program
Katie Ingram	District 5's Behavior Specialist
Nuvong Lee	District 5's Speech-Language Pathologist
James Jerome	LEA Representative
Stanley Young	Vet Tech Professor
Cregg Marchant	Vocational Rehabilitation Representative
JoAnn Peery	St. Joseph's Community College Accessibility Center Liaison

If parent signature is missing, provide a copy of IEP and Procedural Safeguards and check below:

☐ Did not attend (document efforts to involve parent)

☐ Via telephone/video

☐ Other _____

Comments

Describe the Student's Present Levels of Academic Achievement and Functional Performance

IDEA requires that the IEP include a statement of the student's present levels of academic achievement and functional performance (PLAAFP). Stating a student's PLAAFP is the first step in the IEP process because this information is the basis for selecting reasonable goals for the student's improvement over the next year.

WHAT IS A PLAAFP STATEMENT?

A PLAAFP statement is a brief but detailed description of a student's achievement and functional performance at the time the IEP is created. This description is derived from formal and informal assessment conducted by the team, from the student's level of progress on the previous IEP goals, and from consideration of the student's grade-level curriculum standards. The PLAAFP statement must address all areas affected by the disability. Let's take a look at the terms *academic achievement* and *functional performance*.

Academic achievement refers to gaining requisite skills and knowledge for success in school. The most important academic skills students learn are reading, writing, and math because these skills are foundational for achievement in other academic areas such as science, health, and social studies.

Functional performance can be defined as applying knowledge and skills to meet daily needs. Included are social skills such as engaging in healthy relationships and meeting school behavior expectations, as well as adaptive skills such as feeding and dressing oneself, participating in recreational activities, shopping for groceries, and applying and interviewing for a job.

WHY DIFFERENTIATE BETWEEN ACADEMIC ACHIEVEMENT AND FUNCTIONAL PERFORMANCE?

Academic achievement and functional performance are differentiated for students depending on their age and on the effects of disabilities on their learning. Most students' education will focus primarily on the general curriculum, so their PLAAFP statements will center on academic achievement. Other students will need to gain functional living skills along with academic skills; therefore, their PLAAFP statements will describe both functional performance and academic needs.

Generally, the larger the gap between a student's academic or functional performance and age-appropriate core curriculum, the more likely the student's IEP will address functional skills. For example, a five-year-old child who does not correctly identify colors may have an academic goal for obtaining this skill. However, an 18-year-old student who does not correctly identify colors might have a more functional goal to prepare for adult living, such as sorting dark and light colors for laundry.

WHY ARE PLAAFP STATEMENTS IMPORTANT?

PLAAFP statements provide a starting point for all decisions regarding a student's individualized education. Teachers must understand what students know and can do before planning the next steps. For example, if a teacher asks a student to read from *Junie B, First Grader (at last!)* but the student is unable to decode simple words, the result will be frustration and failure. Knowing the student's reading skill level guides the teacher toward an appropriate starting point.

The more accurately the team can describe present levels of academic achievement and functional performance, the more likely they are to plan appropriate annual goals for improvement.

HOW DOES MY TEAM OBTAIN INFORMATION TO DEVELOP A PLAAFP STATEMENT?

Obtaining the necessary information requires three steps: reviewing the curriculum standards for academic achievement, determining the student's current academic strengths and limitations, and assessing the student's current functional strengths and limitations. We describe these below.

1. **Review the curriculum standards for academic achievement.**
   Access your state's curriculum standards and review the requirements for the student's grade level. Because an IEP must provide goals and attendant services required to help the student engage and progress in the general curriculum, the

Standards-Based IEPs

The term *standards-based IEP* refers to PLAAFP statements and associated annual goals developed according to a state's academic curriculum standards. States can either create their own grade-level standards for academic subjects or adopt the Common Core State Standards (National Governors Association Center for Best Practices, Council of Chief State School Officers, 2010).

team should use the grade-level curriculum standards as guideposts to determine the student's goals for improvement. For example, the math common core standard for numbers and operations in base ten states that a third-grade student should "use place value understanding to round whole numbers to the nearest 10 or 100" (CCSS.Math.Content.3.NBT.A.1). This standard will serve as a later example for crafting a PLAAFP statement.

2. **Determine the student's current *academic* strengths and limitations.**
   Multidisciplinary teams use both formal and informal assessment to determine student academic achievement. Formal assessment is typically used to determine eligibility for special education, while informal assessment is used to guide daily instruction.

Formal Assessment

Formal assessments are standardized tests, meaning the assessor follows a prescribed administration protocol for each student; or norm-referenced tests, which compare student achievement to a similar population based on age or grade level; or both. These include tests of intelligence and tests of academic achievement. Intelligence tests broadly measure cognitive aptitude, indicating a student's ability to process information as required for learning, and yield an IQ score.

Common standardized cognitive tests include the *Wechsler Intelligence Scale for Children*, the *Stanford-Binet Intelligence Scales,* and others. Common tests of achievement include the *Woodcock-Johnson Psychoeducational Battery*, the *Wechsler Individual Achievement Test*, the *Kaufman Test of Educational Achievement*, and others. Standardized tests of specific skill areas include *Key Math, Woodcock Diagnostic Reading Battery*, and others.

Informal Assessment

Informal assessment may include criterion-referenced tests, curriculum-based assessments and measures, and teacher or parent checklists. Criterion-referenced tests compare student achievement to set criteria, such as the *Brigance Comprehensive Inventory of Basic Skills, Acadience Reading* (formerly DIBELS Next), some core curriculum tests designed by state offices of education, and alternate assessments designed for students with significant cognitive disabilities. Curriculum-based assessments measure student performance directly from the current curriculum, such as placement tests for a math program, and curriculum-based measures, such as teacher-made tests to systematically check progress toward mastering math facts.

Classroom teachers can provide observational anecdotes, skills checklists, and student work samples to help the team understand a student's strengths and needs. Teachers are also good sources of information about student behavior and interpersonal relations with other students.

Parents or other caregivers are valuable sources of information. They know the student better than the school does and can give insight into interests, hobbies, and talents. Parents can complete behavioral or functional living checklists, and they can also enlighten the team regarding a student's history of success or failure and strategies that have worked well in the past.

Returning to our third-grade common core math example, a team member can use data from a recent formal test or from an informal test with several sample problems to measure a student's ability to use place value understanding to round whole numbers to the nearest 10 or 100. If results show that the student can round to the nearest 10, but not to the nearest 100, then the team will note this performance gap in the PLAAFP statement.

3. **Determine the student's current *functional* strengths and limitations.**
Similar to determining a student's academic performance, the team uses formal and informal assessment along with parent input to identify a student's functional strengths and limitations. Formal assessments of adaptive functioning include norm-referenced tests such as the *Vineland Adaptive Behavior Scales, Scales of Independent Behavior,* and the *Adaptive Behavior Scale.* Other formal assessments measure students' prosocial or maladaptive behavior, such as the *Behavior Observation Sequence* and the *Behavior Assessment System for Children.* These assessments are usually completed by classroom teachers, school psychologists, and/or parents.

Informal assessment involves criterion-referenced tests that compare students' functional skills to set criteria, such as the *Brigance Diagnostic Inventory of Early Development, Checklist of Adaptive Living Skills,* and state or district alternate assessments designed for students with significant cognitive disabilities.

Collaboration with parents is critical when assessing functional skills. Skills that are functional at school may not be functional at home and vice versa, so school professionals and parents must work closely together to describe students' present levels of functional performance across environments.

The team summarizes relevant data from these various sources to describe the student's present levels of academic achievement and functional performance in areas affected by the student's disability. These data are useful for determining the gap between the student's current achievement and relevant standards.

Teaching Functional Skills

It is important to teach functional skills in an environment as close as possible to that in which they will be used. For example, if a parent wants her son to learn to make his bed and the school has no bed for practice, the student is not likely to generalize instruction in bed making from school to home; this skill is better taught in the natural home environment.

HOW DOES MY TEAM CREATE A PLAAFP STATEMENT?

IDEA requires your team to do the following when creating a PLAAFP statement:

1. Describe how the disability affects the student's academic achievement and functional performance in the relevant skill areas.
2. For elementary or secondary students, describe how the disability affects the student's involvement and progress in the general education curriculum.
3. For preschool students, as appropriate, describe how the disability affects the student's participation in appropriate activities.

In practice, teams often include a statement of the student's strengths as well as the effects of the disability on the individual's achievement or functional performance. This strengths-based approach more accurately portrays the student's functioning by stating what he or she has mastered within the curriculum. The common format for this type of PLAAFP statement has three parts, focused in reference to relevant standards:

1. A description of the student's academic or functional strengths, sometimes referred to as "can do"
2. A description of the student's academic or functional limitations, or "cannot do"
3. A statement of needed improvement to progress in the general curriculum, or "needs to"

A well-written PLAAFP statement has sufficient detail to provide descriptive and logical cues for writing the accompanying annual goals.

WHAT IF THE DEMANDS OF THE GENERAL CURRICULUM ARE TOO HIGH FOR SOME STUDENTS?

IDEA recognizes that a few students' disabilities are likely to prevent them from meeting grade-level standards in the general curriculum even with appropriate accommodations and modifications (34 CFR §300.320[a][2][ii]). All students are required to take state assessments to meet accountability standards of the *Every Student Succeeds Act* (ESSA; 2018). However, ESSA states that up to 1% of a state or district's students (approximately 10% of students with disabilities) may take alternate assessments aligned to state-approved alternate achievement standards (34 CFR §200.13[c][2][ii]). IEP teams decide which students will take standard assessments, with or without modifications or accommodations, and which students will take alternate assessments. You will learn more about this in Step 6.

Alternate achievement standards, sometimes referred to as *extended standards*, are created and adopted by individual states. ESSA requires states to link alternate standards to the grade-level core standards; they may be reduced in breadth or depth, but they must be appropriately challenging. For example, Dynamic Learning Maps Essential Elements (EE; University of Kansas, 2010) alternate standards indicate that where the first grade common core requires students to decode regularly spelled one-syllable words (RF.1.3), students with significant cognitive disabilities will with guidance and support recognize familiar words that are used in everyday routines (EE.RF 1.3; Utah State Board of Education, n.d.). Alternate achievement standards are the reference for developing academic PLAAFP statements for these students.

WHAT DOES A PLAAFP STATEMENT LOOK LIKE?

Here is the PLAAFP statement for reading for our second grade student with learning disabilities named Rajesh:

> Woodcock-Johnson IV Tests of Cognitive Abilities© given 1/21/__ indicate Rajesh functions in the normal range of cognitive abilities. Woodcock-Johnson IV Tests of Achievement© (1/22/__) show that Rajesh can say the alphabet by rote. He cannot count, pronounce, blend, or segment syllables in spoken words. He does not associate long and short vowel sounds with common spellings or read common high frequency words by sight at the first-grade level. To progress in the Grade 2 curriculum, Rajesh needs to know and apply grade-level phonics and word analysis skills in decoding words (CCSS.ELA-Literacy.RF2.3) and read with sufficient accuracy and fluency to support comprehension (CCSS.ELA-Literacy.RF2.4).

DOES RAJESH'S PLAAFP INCLUDE THE NECESSARY ELEMENTS?

Yes, it does, but let's take a closer look at the statement to see *how* it includes the necessary elements:

1. It describes how the disability affects the student's academic achievement and functional performance in the relevant skill areas.

   Rajesh can say the alphabet by rote. He cannot count, pronounce, blend, or segment syllables in spoken words. He does not associate long and short vowel sounds with common spellings or read common high frequency words by sight at the first-grade level.

2. It states how the disability affects the student's engagement and progress in the general education curriculum.

To progress in the Grade 2 curriculum, Rajesh needs to know and apply grade-level phonics and word analysis skills in decoding words (CCSS.ELA-Literacy.RF2.3) and read with sufficient accuracy and fluency to support comprehension (CCSS. ELA-Literacy.RF2.4).

3. If this IEP was for a preschool student, it would state, as appropriate, how the disability affects the student's participation in appropriate activities.

This does not apply to Rajesh because he is in the second grade.

MAY I SEE ANOTHER EXAMPLE?

Sure. Here is the math PLAAFP statement from Keej's IEP, which does not reference the core curriculum because he is one of the few students whose significant cognitive disabilities are best addressed with an alternate curriculum:

MATH: Informal assessment (January 12–16) indicates that Keej can use Excel spreadsheets to enter data into rows and columns, but he can use the "function" feature for addition, subtraction, multiplication, and division with only 45% accuracy, a skill that is required for a vet tech to prepare invoices and record inventory. He measures volume using standard units of measurement with 50% accuracy, a skill that is necessary for disinfecting instruments, preparing cleaning solutions, and completing other related tasks in the vet tech lab. Keej uses Venmo, PayPal, and his bank debit card to make monetary transactions; however, he misplaces the decimal point approximately 55% of the time, resulting in inaccurate, and sometimes costly, transactions.

Although he has interest and emerging proficiency in these areas, his levels of accuracy and independence in these areas of math affect his ability to reach his post-secondary goals. Keej needs to solve real-world problems involving addition and subtraction of decimals (EE.N-CN.2.b [Essential Elements alternate curriculum]), measure liquid volumes using standard units (EE.4.MD.2.b), and make monetary transactions including decimals (EE.N-CN.2.b) with at least 80% accuracy.

DOES KEEJ'S EXAMPLE INCLUDE THE NECESSARY ELEMENTS?

Yes, it does, but let's look closely at the statement so you can see how it includes the necessary elements for a student with significant cognitive disabilities whose needs fall within an alternate academic curriculum:

1. It describes how the disability affects the student's academic achievement and functional performance in the relevant skill areas.

Keej can use Excel spreadsheets to enter data into rows and columns, but he can use the "function" feature for addition, subtraction, multiplication, and division with only 45% accuracy, a skill that is required for a vet tech to prepare invoices and record inventory. He measures volume using standard units of measurement with 50% accuracy, a skill that is necessary for disinfecting instruments, preparing cleaning solutions, and completing other related tasks in the vet tech lab. Keej uses Venmo, PayPal, and his bank debit card to make monetary transactions; however, he misplaces the decimal point approximately 55% of the time, resulting in inaccurate, and sometimes costly transactions.

2. It states how the disability affects the student's involvement and progress in the general education curriculum.

   Keej is 19 years old; there is no general curriculum for post-secondary students. He is learning from an alternative curriculum suited to his functional needs.

3. If this IEP was for a preschool student, it would state, as appropriate, how the disability affects the student's participation in appropriate activities.

   This does not apply to Keej because he is in a post-secondary program.

WHAT ABOUT PLAAFP STATEMENTS FOR STUDENTS WITH BEHAVIORAL NEEDS?

Behavioral expectations are not usually listed as hierarchical standards like academics, so team members must identify and define student behaviors that are and are not appropriate and productive in various settings. Teams use observation data summarized as detailed descriptions of behavior to create appropriate PLAAFP statements. Observation formats describe behaviors, such as "in seat," "out of seat," "talk outs," "hitting," and "noncompliance with teacher directives," and record frequency, duration, and/or latency data to define the number or degree of occurrences.

Teams must use multiple observations over different days, times, and environments to determine if student behavior is pervasive, contextual, or if the student is having an occasional bad day. IEPs should address measurable behaviors that consistently interfere with the student's progress in the general curriculum or interfere with the learning of other students.

MY MENTOR Having a few bad behavior days is not the same as having serious emotional disturbance. Sometimes things just don't go well for kids.

MAY I SEE AN EXAMPLE?

Sure. Let's look at Phoebe's PLAAFP statement addressing her behavior:

Adult observations on 9/30/__, 10/14/__, 10/27/__, 12/3/__, and 1/22/__ show that Phoebe engages in assigned tasks about 10% of opportunities. She initiates or participates in conversation with peers 0% of opportunities. Same age and gender peers in her classes engage in tasks 90% of opportunities and initiate or participate in conversations 95% of opportunities. To progress in the general curriculum Phoebe needs to ask for task assistance when needed. To develop appropriate social skills she needs to participate in peer conversations.

Notice that Phoebe's PLAAFP describes these behaviors:

- *Engages in assigned tasks*
- *Initiates or participates in conversation with peers*

The IEP also includes how the behavior was measured:

- *Adult observations on 9/30/__, 10/14/__, 10/27/__, 12/3/__, and 1/22/__*

It notes the percentage of engagement:

- *about 10% of opportunities*
- *0% of opportunities*

And it includes two "needs to" statements

- *needs to ask for task assistance when needed*
- *needs to participate in peer conversations*

NOW IT'S YOUR TURN

Here are assessment data for Samuel, a fourth-grade student with intellectual disabilities who is learning from the general curriculum. Your task is to summarize the data into a brief but descriptive PLAAFP for Samuel's IEP. When you have finished, check your PLAAFP with our suggestion in the appendix.

Achievement Testing

- **Math Calculation:** 9/10 one-digit addition and subtraction correct; 0/10 two-digit and one-digit without renaming correct; 0/5 multiplication and division correct.
- **Written expression:** Dictates simple sentences when given a subject, 5/5 correct; writes simple sentences when given a subject, 0/5 correct.

Functional Skills Assessment

- **Self-Help Skills:** Correctly selects his backpack in a group of others, but does not place school materials in the backpack without prompting. Uses the restroom independently, but does not fasten pants or wash hands without reminding.
- **Socialization:** Starts, joins, and maintains a conversation with peers, but does not end a conversation without prompting; interrupts others in their conversations.

Step 1 • Describe the Student's Present Levels of Academic Achievement . . .

PLAAFP for Samuel

Assessment indicates Samuel can _____

_____

_____

_____

He cannot _____

_____

_____

To progress in the general curriculum Samuel needs to _____

_____

_____

_____

COMMON ERRORS

Here are errors that are common in writing PLAAFP statements:

1. Writing a statement with vague descriptions of achievement or performance
   "Sophia is earning a C– in math."
   "Emma's reading standard score is 84."
   "Mason can't control his behaviors in public."

2. Writing a statement that is not related to the student's curriculum
   "Ava is very helpful at home."
   "Maya is a conscientious teacher's helper."
   "Noah eats his breakfast without assistance."

3. Writing a statement that is not related to the student's disability
   "Luis [with a reading disability] has excellent grades in band and chorus."
   "Yulia [five-year-old with a speech fluency disorder] knows her colors and shapes."

4. Writing a "can do" statement but no "cannot" or "does not do" statement
   "Leilani knows her letter names and sounds and can sound out simple words."
   "Sangeetha behaves appropriately in a well-structured setting."
   "Billi has learned to ride the bus independently."

5. For a preschooler, writing a statement that does not indicate how the disability affects the student's participation in appropriate activities.

"Francesco [three years old] is unable to state his birth date." (Most three-year-olds cannot do this, so it is not an appropriate activity.)

"Cyrus [four years old] cannot sit for more than 30 minutes to listen to the teacher read a story." (Four-year-olds are not expected to sit and listen for 30 minutes, so this is not an appropriate activity.)

"Quon [four years old] is unable to match upper- and lowercase letters on a worksheet." (Four-year-olds generally do not use worksheets, and the task is too complex for her age, so this is not an appropriate activity.)

NOW YOU TRY SOME

For each incomplete or poorly written PLAAFP statement below, indicate the common errors. Check your answers with ours in the appendix.

PLAAFP statement: *"Kingston [14-year-old boy] initiates and sustains conversations with peers and can call his friends on the telephone."*

Error: _____

_____

PLAAFP statement: *"Evangeline [nine-year-old girl with specific learning disabilities in reading] writes all uppercase and lowercase letters in isolation and in words. She does not form closed letters correctly. Her penmanship skills inhibit her progress in the general writing curriculum."*

Error: _____

_____

PLAAFP statement: *"McCoy [six-year-old boy] is often out of control and is unhappy with school."*

Error: _____

_____

LET'S REVIEW THE ELEMENTS OF A PLAAFP STATEMENT

A PLAAFP statement must include these three elements:

1. A description of how the disability affects the student's academic achievement and functional performance in relevant skill areas
2. For K–12 students, a statement of how the disability affects the student's involvement and progress in the general education curriculum
3. For preschool students, as appropriate, an explanation of how the disability affects the student's participation in appropriate activities

Step 1 • Describe the Student's Present Levels of Academic Achievement . . .

In practice the PLAAFP may include these elements referencing relevant standards:

1. A description of the student's strengths, sometimes referred to as "can do"
2. A description of the student's limitations, or "cannot do"
3. A statement of needed improvement to progress in the general curriculum, or "needs to"

The statement should look like this for a student with academic needs:

Duncan [second grade] **can** say all letter names and sounds. Acadience testing of 1/21/15 shows that he **cannot** read second-grade oral reading passages at the mid-year benchmark of 72 wcpm. He cannot answer literal or inferential reading comprehension questions from Acadience oral reading fluency passages. He **needs to** read with sufficient accuracy and fluency to support comprehension to progress in the general curriculum. (CCSS.ELA.LITERACY.RF.2.4)

 Congratulations! You have completed Step 1. Let's move on to **Step 2,** writing measurable annual goals.

✔ Describe the student's present levels of academic achievement and functional performance.

STEP 2 Write measurable annual goals.

STEP 3 Measure and report student progress.

STEP 4 State the services needed to achieve annual goals.

STEP 5 Explain the extent, if any, to which the student will not participate with nondisabled students in the regular class and in extracurricular and other nonacademic activities.

STEP 6 Explain accommodations necessary to measure academic achievement and functional performance on state and district-wide assessments.

STEP 7 Complete a transition plan for students aged 16 and older.

References

National Governors Association Center for Best Practices, Council of Chief State School Officers. (2010). *Common Core State Standards*. http://www.corestandards.org

University of Kansas. (2010). *Dynamic Learning Maps Essential Elements*. Lawrence, KS: Center for Educational Testing & Evaluation. http://dynamiclearningmaps. org/content/essential-elements

Utah State Board of Education. (n.d.). *Teaching the Essential Elements to students with significant cognitive disabilities*. https://www.schools.utah.gov/file/602ec10c-681e-4725-b9b9-d4452c549637

STEP 2

Write Measurable Annual Goals

You have learned that statements of a student's present levels of academic achievement and functional performance describe how the disability affects involvement and progress in the general education curriculum. In this step, you will learn that measurable annual goals designate what the student is expected to achieve within one year to address the effects of the disability. Present levels reflect current performance; annual goals describe future achievement.

WHAT ARE MEASURABLE ANNUAL GOALS?

Measurable annual goals are the IEP team's best estimate of what the student can accomplish in the next year. A statement of measurable academic and functional performance goals must do the following:

1. Meet the student's needs related to the disability that may interfere with his or her involvement and progress in the general education curriculum.
2. Meet the student's additional educational needs resulting from the disability.
3. Be measurable.

WHAT IS THE GENERAL EDUCATION CURRICULUM?

The general curriculum is established by a state office of education and implemented in individual schools under the direction of school districts. Some states provide curricula consisting of a general scope and sequence for each grade level, while others use more specific measurable outcomes for each subject area in each grade. Most states participate in the Common Core State Standards Initiative, which is the reference for the sample goals in this chapter and in our sample IEPs. It is important to know that all students with disabilities are entitled to have access to and progress in the general curriculum like their peers without disabilities.

WHAT ARE "ADDITIONAL EDUCATIONAL NEEDS RESULTING FROM THE DISABILITY"?

IDEA requires teams to consider a student's academic, developmental, and functional needs. Because the designation general education curriculum refers mainly to academic subjects, "additional educational needs" refers to the student's developmental and functional needs that result directly from the disability. The term *developmental* refers to a predictable sequence of growth. Therefore, a student with developmental difficulties may fall considerably behind peers in such areas as self-care, language, or motor skills. *Functional* refers to applying knowledge and skills to meet every day needs such as eating, dressing, communicating, and accessing transportation. The curriculum for a preschool child with severe disabilities may focus on developmental growth, whereas an adolescent's curriculum may focus on functional living skills.

WHAT DOES "MEASURABLE" MEAN?

Measurable means the behavior stated in the goal can be observed and measured to determine when it has been achieved. For example, a goal to understand addition is not observable or measurable because it does not specify how the student will demonstrate understanding. You cannot watch a student understand; you can only see evidence of understanding in some observable form. Stated in measurable terms, the goal might be "write correct answers to addition problems." You can observe written answers and easily measure their accuracy.

HOW DOES THE IEP TEAM SET GOALS THAT ARE IMPORTANT TO THE STUDENT AND THE FAMILY?

The team sets goals that are important to the student and the family by inviting and considering their desires and opinions. You'll remember that the IEP team includes the parents or guardians, relevant school professionals, and the student when appropriate. Each team member contributes necessary perspectives toward setting appropriate goals, and parent and student perspectives are very important. Let's look at each team member's contributions.

Parents. Parents know much about what the student can reasonably accomplish, based on their child's history in the home and at school. Thus, IEP teams must consider and include parent perspectives in goal setting. Too often parents are marginalized in the goal-setting process by school personnel who are more concerned with having the student fit in with existing curricula and convenient routines than with what is actually most appropriate.

Regular classroom teacher. The regular classroom teacher understands the general curriculum and can guide the team to align IEP goals with it.

Special education teacher. The special education teacher can break down the general curriculum standards or instructional tasks in the areas affected by the student's disability in order to write reasonable goals for achievement within the year.

Related service providers. Related service providers include professionals such as speech-language pathologists, occupational therapists, physical therapists, school psychologists, and school social workers. These professionals provide assessment information in their areas of specialty to help the team develop goals for improvement in the specialty areas they represent.

Individual(s) who can interpret evaluation results. A teacher or related services provider who can explain test results should be included so that team members can understand the results and apply them in selecting appropriate goals. For example, a special education teacher can interpret achievement test results, a school psychologist can explain psychological test results, and an occupational therapist can explain the results of fine motor skill assessments.

Local education agency (LEA) representative. The LEA representative verifies the availability of resources necessary to achieve the goals. The LEA representative may be the principal, assistant principal, other school administrator or designee.

Other individuals with special knowledge or expertise. At the discretion of the parent or the school, participants in goal setting may include a family advocate, a cultural/linguistic interpreter, an after-school care provider, or other individual who has relevant knowledge of the disability or of the child as an individual.

Student. Student participation in goal setting helps the team understand personal likes, dislikes, and goals for the future, particularly when the IEP team begins to plan for the student's transition to adult life. Students should be invited to take part in the IEP planning when they are able to contribute.

SHOULD IEP GOALS ADDRESS GRADE-LEVEL STANDARDS?

Not necessarily. The U. S. Supreme Court recently decided in the Endrew F. v. Douglas County School District Re-1 case that not all students will have IEP goals for grade-level achievement. Instead, the IEP team must create goals that will drive as much improvement as is "appropriately ambitious for students, in light of their circumstances" (Endrew F. v. Douglas County School District Re-1, 2017).

HOW DO I WRITE GRADE-LEVEL GOALS WHEN THE STUDENT'S ACHIEVEMENT IS WELL BELOW GRADE LEVEL?

When the student is achieving well below grade level, the team might write goals using a bi-level approach. The bi-level approach means that one or more goals address the student's grade-level core standards and one or more goals address necessary skill improvements at a lower level. For example, for a student who cannot read on grade level the team may consider the student's strengths that can contribute to grade-level goals without requiring reading skills the student does not have. On a lower level, subsequent goals can address the skill deficits within the same standard (Yates, 2014).

CAN I SEE EXAMPLES OF BI-LEVEL ANNUAL GOALS?

Sure. Let's look at Rajesh, who is in second grade. His third reading goal is "Given literature passages at second-grade level read orally, and weekly opportunities to practice, Rajesh will use information gained from words in a print or digital text to tell the characters, setting, or plot (CCSS.ELA-LITERACY.RL2.7) with 90% accuracy as measured by teacher observation records." The common core standard actually requires students to "read" and comprehend, but Rajesh cannot read second-grade reading passages yet.

Therefore, his third goal addresses comprehension through listening to the passages and then answering questions by telling. This grade-level goal still addresses the comprehension requirement, but it does not rely on reading. Goals 1 and 2 address skill deficits for reading fluency and reading comprehension at his second-grade level.

Remember, the PLAAFP statement includes "can do," "cannot do," and "needs to" statements. The "needs to" statement identifies the grade-level standard, and the "cannot do" statements indicate skill deficits that need improvement. Therefore, begin by writing a goal for the "needs to" grade-level curriculum standard and then write goals to address the "cannot do" skill deficit(s). Let's look at the reading example from Rajesh's IEP.

PLAAFP

Woodcock-Johnson IV Tests of Cognitive Abilities© given 1/21/__ indicate Rajesh functions in the normal range of cognitive abilities. Woodcock-Johnson IV Tests of Achievement© (1/22/__) show that Rajesh can say the alphabet by rote. He cannot count, pronounce, blend, or segment syllables in spoken words. He does not associate long and short vowel sounds with common spellings or read common high frequency words by sight at the first-grade level. To progress in the Grade 2 curriculum, Rajesh needs to know and apply grade-level phonics and word analysis skills in decoding words (CCSS.ELA-Literacy.RF2.3) and read with sufficient accuracy and fluency to support comprehension (CCSS.ELA-Literacy.RF2.4).

Goal Indicators

The "needs to" part of the PLAFFP statement indicates what should be addressed in the annual goal(s).

Needs to. Rajesh needs to know and apply grade-level phonics and word analysis skills in decoding words (CCSS.ELA-Literacy.RF2.3) and read with sufficient accuracy and fluency to support comprehension (CCSS.ELA-Literacy.RF2.4).

1. **Annual Goal**

   Given second-grade one- and two-syllable regularly and irregularly spelled words and weekly opportunities to practice, Rajesh will read the words correctly with at least 95% accuracy, as measured by teacher observation records (CCSS.ELA-LITERACY.RF2.3).

   Cannot do. Rajesh cannot count, pronounce, blend, or segment syllables in spoken words.

2. **Annual Goal**

   Given passages at first-grade level from literature and weekly opportunities to practice, Rajesh will read at least 72 words correct per minute and answer such questions as *who, what, where, when, why*, and *how* to demonstrate understanding of key details in a text (CCSS.ELA-LITERACY.RL2.1) with 90% accuracy as measured by progress monitoring.

   Cannot do. Rajesh cannot read common high frequency words by sight at the first-grade level.

3. Annual Goal

Given literature passages at second-grade level read orally and weekly opportunities to practice, Rajesh will use information gained from words in a print or digital text to tell the characters, setting, or plot (CCSS.ELA-LITERACY. RL2.7) with 90% accuracy as measured by teacher observation records.

Notice the bi-level nature of the goals. The first goal addresses the grade-level standard for word identification. The second goal requires reading and comprehending, but at the first-grade level. The third annual goal requires listening rather than reading comprehension and telling answers rather than writing. Given appropriately intensive instruction and practice, it is not unreasonable for Rajesh to attain grade- or near grade-level in reading achievement.

WHAT ARE THE COMPONENTS OF A MEASURABLE ANNUAL GOAL?

IDEA does not specify the wording for writing a measurable annual goal. The law requires only that annual goals must address progress in the general curriculum, address other needs caused by the disability, and be measurable. IEP teams usually use a format established by the school or district. In addition, best practice suggests that a truly measurable goal has at least four elements.

1. **The student's name.** Including the student's name personalizes the goal and assures that anyone accessing the record knows whose needs are addressed.
2. **A description of the conditions under which the behavior will be performed.** Conditions may include instructional personnel, materials, settings, and specific instructional cues. The conditions for Rajesh's second annual goal are "given passages at first-grade level from literature and weekly opportunities to practice."
3. **The specific observable behavior to be performed.** This designated behavior should come from the PLAAFP statement. Observable behaviors are those the teacher can see or hear. For example, the behavior for Rajesh's third annual goal is to "use information gained from words in a print or digital text to tell the characters, setting, or plot." The teacher can hear Rajesh read but would not be able to observe how he understands, thinks, or feels about reading simply by listening. *Understands, thinks, feels,* and *knows* are not observable behaviors; therefore, these terms should not be used in writing annual goals. Similarly, the phrase "be able to" is not appropriate for the annual goal, for two reasons. First, students may be able to engage in certain behaviors but be prevented from doing so by conditions, such as lack of access to materials or insufficient time to complete tasks. Second, the wording is imprecise: The word *will* is more active and direct.
4. **The criterion to indicate the level of performance at which the goal will be achieved.** The criterion for Rajesh's third goal is "with 90% accuracy." This means that he will answer at least 90% of comprehension questions correctly from assigned reading passages. Criteria must be related to the behavior. There are many ways to set criteria:

- *Percentage* is appropriate where the number of trials differs from time to time, such as 80% of all opportunities to engage in peer play.
- *Number correct* or *number of allowable errors* is used when the number of trials remains constant, such as 20 out of 25 spelling words each week, or fewer than five errors.
- *Rate* refers to speed and accuracy, such as 70 words read correctly in one minute or 55 math facts written correctly in one minute.
- *Frequency* is a measure of the number of times a behavior occurs in a set time frame, such as the number of verbal outbursts in a 50-minute class period.
- *Latency* measures the time lapse between a stimulus and the desired student response. For instance, the criterion may require a student to respond to a peer's greeting within 15 seconds.
- *Duration* indicates the length of time a behavior continues, such as a student staying on task for 10 minutes before getting distracted.

The appropriate criterion measure for a goal is an important choice. For example, a teacher once collected frequency data on student crying that showed that the student cried only twice per day: once from 8:00 a.m. until lunchtime and once from lunch until 3:00 p.m. The teacher soon realized that duration data were more appropriate.

CONSIDER ADDING TWO COMPONENTS TO THE ANNUAL GOAL

Often, students with disabilities experience difficulty performing the required tasks under different conditions. You may have heard one teacher say, "He is such an angel in my class" while another teacher says "he is always acting up!" This shows that the conditions under which the student is behaving differ and the student has not "generalized" the behavior to different settings or people. Similarly, you may have heard a teacher report that a student can count to 10 accurately on Friday, but is unable to do so on the following Monday. This points to the difficulty some students have maintaining a previously learned skill. Therefore, adding statements about generalization and maintenance is important for students who struggle in these areas.

1. **A statement of generalization indicating additional conditions under which the behavior will be performed to criterion.** Generalization criteria insure that the student can perform the task under various circumstances, including
   - with different people,
   - in various environments,
   - with varied instructional cues,
   - across times of day, and
   - with different materials.

   For example, Keej's career/vocational benchmarks require him to complete a work task with varied instructional cues: picture/audio prompts, then audio prompts, then without prompts.

2. **A statement of maintenance indicating the student will perform the task to criterion for a specified period of time.** This is appropriate when the skill needs to be performed accurately over a period of time in order to assure mastery. The student may need more opportunities to practice the skill with high levels of accuracy to ensure retention. Maintenance data need not be collected daily once the student has reached mastery criterion. Teachers may measure maintenance by probing, or collecting data, on a weekly or monthly basis. For example, the maintenance statement for Keej's math benchmarks requires him to "maintain the skill when probed weekly for at least four weeks," which will demonstrate that he has both mastered and retained each of the skills.

WHY DOES BEST PRACTICE INCLUDE THESE ELEMENTS FOR ANNUAL GOALS?

These six elements ensure that all team members understand and agree on the specific learning or behaviors expected of a student. This is essential for three reasons:

1. Teachers use well written goals to plan accurate instruction and learning activities for students. Nebulous or nonspecific annual goals are too likely to lead to undirected instruction and wasted learning time.
2. Teachers use these elements to design and administer accurate assessments of student progress toward the annual goals. Continual monitoring guides teachers to make changes in curriculum and instruction if a student is not progressing.
3. Team members refer to the components of well written annual goals to verify the student's final achievement.

MAY I SEE EXAMPLES OF POORLY WRITTEN ANNUAL GOALS?

Certainly. Here are two examples that omit important elements.

Example 1: *Edgar will understand how to write accurately.*

YES (NO) statement of conditions in which the behavior will be performed
YES (NO) statement of observable, measurable behavior
YES (NO) statement of criterion for mastery
YES (NO) statement of generalization
YES (NO) statement of maintenance

Example 2: *When asked by the teacher, Katya will behave appropriately for three consecutive weeks.*

(YES) NO a statement of conditions in which behavior will be performed
YES (NO) statement of observable, measurable behavior
YES (NO) statement of criterion for mastery
YES (NO) statement of generalization
(YES) NO a statement of maintenance

NOW IT'S YOUR TURN

1. Here is an annual goal for Maddie. Write the phrase from the goal next to the matching element in the list below. Then check your answer with our suggestions in the appendix.

Annual Goal

When given a grocery list with five or fewer items and a $10.00 bill, Maddie will select and purchase all the items on the list with fewer than five prompts in different grocery stores over a three-week period.

Conditions	Student	Behavior	Criteria	Generalization	Maintenance

2. Here is one part of a PLAAPF statement for Suraj, a second-grade boy. Your task is to write an annual goal to address this need, making sure to include all five elements. Check your answer with the appendix.

PLAAPF Statement

When directed by the teacher to be seated, Suraj yells defiantly and refuses to sit at his desk 80% of observed instances across settings.

Annual Goal

Conditions	Student	Behavior	Criteria	Generalization	Maintenance

Each IEP team might create annual goals that differ from the goals written by other teams, based on the team's knowledge of the student's preferences and capabilities and the demands of the educational environments in which the student is served. So, the goals we suggest in the appendix serve only as examples of what a team might decide is appropriate for Maddie and Suraj.

DOES THE IEP TEAM NEED TO BREAK DOWN THE ANNUAL GOALS INTO SUBGOALS FOR MY STUDENTS?

This requirement varies. Subgoals are often broken down into benchmarks or short-term objectives, which we explain below. Previous versions of IDEA required that all annual goals include benchmarks or short-term objectives. Now the law requires these provisions only for students who take alternate assessments aligned to alternate achievement standards.

WHAT DOES THIS MEAN FOR THE TEAM?

The IEP team must determine a student's need for alternate assessments aligned to alternate achievement standards and then add benchmarks or short-term objectives to the annual goals. Alternate standards/assessments procedures apply only to the small percentage of students whose disabilities inhibit them from progressing comparably to their peers without disabilities in the general curriculum; these students cannot be held to the same standards.

WHAT ARE BENCHMARKS AND SHORT-TERM OBJECTIVES?

Benchmarks and short-term objectives are two ways to break down annual goals into smaller measurable parts. They enable teachers to monitor student achievement in intervals and report progress to IEP team members more than once per year. The two terms are often used interchangeably, but we see benchmarks and short-term objectives as different ways to describe expected intermediate progress toward annual goals.

Benchmarks, which are concerned with a single skill, have three components:

1. They break down one skill into major milestones to be achieved sequentially.
2. They describe levels of increasing performance for the target skill, such as accuracy, fluency, difficulty, or quality.
3. Many of them include dates by which students are expected to meet the milestones.

For example, a student walking from her classroom to the cafeteria requires that she proceed to the first hallway, continue to the second hallway, and so on until she arrives at the cafeteria. Her goal is to travel from her classroom to the school cafeteria, and the turns represent benchmarks that must be met accurately and sequentially.

Short-term objectives describe multiple related but distinct and nonsequential skills necessary to achieve the annual goal. For example, preparing to travel from the classroom to the cafeteria might require the student to put away her books, wash her hands, get her lunch ticket, and get her jacket. These tasks are related to preparing to go to the cafeteria but need not be completed in a particular sequence.

WOULD YOU EXPLAIN THE TERMS AND ACCOMPANYING PROCESSES IN MORE DETAIL?

Certainly.

Benchmarks

Benchmarks set out major milestones to achieving an annual goal. These goals can be broken down into benchmarks in a variety of ways, including performance, assistance level, task analysis, and generalization. See Figure 3. Here are some sample phrases from benchmarks showing these four ways to break down annual goals.

Performance. The goal can be benchmarked according to within-child factors like the level of accuracy, fluency, difficulty, or quality required to ensure that the student has acquired the skill or knowledge.

- Wash, dry, and put away kitchen utensils in the correct sequence at least 67% correctly by October 31. (accuracy)
- Read 50 words correctly per minute by January 31 and 70 words correctly per minute by March 31. (fluency)
- Put on shoes by December 10; then put on shoes and fasten Velcro by February 1; and finally, put on shoes, then tie shoelaces by May 15. (difficulty)
- Write numerals 0 through 9 in order with correct form, slant, and spacing by February 15. (quality)

FIGURE 3 Benchmarks: Performance.

This example shows the "needs to" portion of a Present Levels of Academic Achievement and Functional Performance (PLAAFP) statement, followed by the annual goal divided into benchmarks with projected achievement dates with three criteria for increased accuracy throughout the school year.

PLAAFP "Needs to" Statement	Benchmark 1	Benchmark 2	Annual Goal
	Increased accuracy, fluency, difficulty, or quality	Increased accuracy, fluency, difficulty, or quality	Increased accuracy, fluency, difficulty, or quality
Student needs to read 2.5 grade level fiction and nonfiction text with 80% accuracy.	Read 2.5 level fiction and nonfiction text with **40%** accuracy by Dec.1	Read 2.5 level fiction and nonfiction text with **60%** accuracy by Mar.1	Read 2.5 level fiction and nonfiction text with **80%** accuracy by Jun.1

Assistance level. The goal can be benchmarked according to the level of outside assistance needed to complete the task. See Figure 4. An example of this progressive assistance level follows:

- Use a computer mouse with full physical prompting in 10 weeks.
- Use a computer mouse with only verbal prompting in 15 weeks.
- Use a computer mouse with no prompting in 20 weeks.

FIGURE 4 Benchmarks: Assistance Level.

This example shows the "needs to" portion of a Present Levels of Academic Achievement and Functional Performance (PLAAFP) statement, followed by the annual goal divided into benchmarks with projected achievement dates showing four ways to provide decreasing levels of assistance throughout the school year.

PLAAFP "Needs to" Statement	Benchmark 1	Benchmark 2	Benchmark 3	Annual Goal
Student needs to complete dressing tasks without prompting.	Full prompt — Complete dressing tasks with **full physical prompting** by Oct. 1	Partial prompt — Complete dressing tasks with **partial physical prompting** by Dec. 1	Model — Complete dressing tasks with **modeling** by Feb. 1	No prompt — Complete dressing tasks with **no prompting** by Apr. 1

Task analysis. The goal can be task analyzed: broken down into components to be mastered sequentially in order to accomplish the complete goal. See Figure 5. For example, the goal of counting to 100 could use these benchmarks:

- Rote count 1–10 in five weeks.
- Rote count 1–20 (requires teen numbers) in eight weeks.
- Rote count 1–100 (uses the same pattern after 20) in 15 weeks.

Generalization. A goal can be benchmarked by increasing areas of generalization to other people, environments, instructional cues, times of day, and/or materials. See Figure 6. For example, the IEP team may choose to benchmark an IEP goal to totally care for toileting needs with the most salient form(s) of generalization.

- Totally care for toileting needs while other students are and are not in the school restroom by November 1. (people)
- Totally care for toileting needs using various restrooms in the community by April 1. (environment)
- Totally care for toileting needs when reminded by the teacher and when shown a picture prompt by October 15. (instructional cue)
- Totally care for toileting needs before and after lunch by February 28. (time of day)
- Totally care for toileting needs using a toilet and urinal by March 30. (materials)

FIGURE 5   Benchmarks: Task Analysis.

This example shows the "needs to" portion of a Present Levels of Academic Achievement and Functional Performance (PLAAFP) statement, followed by the annual goal divided into benchmarks with projected achievement dates showing four sequential steps necessary to meet the annual goal.

				Annual Goal
			Benchmark 3	Skill 4 **Fold** clothes by May 1
		Benchmark 2	Skill 3 **Dry** clothes by Feb.1	Skill 3 Dry clothes
	Benchmark 1	Skill 2 **Wash** clothes by Dec.1	Skill 2 Wash clothes	Skill 2 Wash clothes
PLAAFP "Needs to" Statement	Skill 1 **Sort** clothes by Oct.1	Skill 1 Sort clothes	Skill 1 Sort clothes	Skill 1 Sort clothes
Student needs to sort, wash, dry and fold clothes.				

FIGURE 6   Benchmarks: Generalization.

This example shows the "needs to" portion of a Present Levels of Academic Achievement and Functional Performance (PLAAFP) statement, followed by the annual goal divided into benchmarks with projected achievement dates showing three ways to generalize the skill across the school year. It also shows the annual goal broken down into two rather than three short-term objectives.

			Annual Goal
		Benchmark 2	3 Different persons, environments, cues, times, and/or materials Purchase food from **street vendor** by May 1
	Benchmark 1	2 Different persons, environments, cues, times, and/or materials Purchase food in **sit-down restaurant** by Feb.1	Purchase food in sit-down restaurant
PLAAFP "Needs to" Statement	1 Person, environment, cue, time, and/or material Purchase food in **fast-food restaurant** by Nov.1	Purchase food in fast-food restaurant	Purchase food in fast-food restaurant
Student needs to purchase food in fast-food restaurants, in sit-down restaurants, and from street vendors.			

These criteria are not mutually exclusive. You may decide to combine two or more of them in writing benchmarks for annual goals. See Figure 7.

FIGURE 7   Benchmarks: Combination of Performance and Assistance Level.

This example shows the "needs to" portion of a Present Levels of Academic Achievement and Functional Performance (PLAAFP) statement. The annual goal is divided into benchmarks with projected achievement dates with increasing criteria for accuracy combined with levels of decreasing assistance throughout the school year.

PLAAFP "Needs to" Statement	Benchmark 1	Benchmark 2	Benchmark 3	Annual Goal
Student needs to follow picture-based directions with at least 80% accuracy without assistance.	Increased accuracy, fluency, difficulty, or quality Follow picture-based directions, **60%** accuracy, **full physical prompts** by Nov. 1	Increased accuracy, fluency, difficulty, or quality Follow picture-based directions, **70%** accuracy, **partial physical prompts** by Feb. 1	Increased accuracy, fluency, difficulty, or quality Follow picture-based directions, **80%** accuracy, **peer modeling** by Apr. 1	Increased accuracy, fluency, difficulty, or quality Follow picture-based directions, **80%** accuracy, **no assistance** by Jun. 1

How many benchmarks must the team write?

The law uses the plural terminology "a description of benchmarks or short-term objectives"; thus, there must be at least two benchmarks for each annual goal.

MAY I SEE AN EXAMPLE OF A GOAL WITH BENCHMARKS?

Here is an example of benchmarks for Keej using task analysis (See Figure 8):

Annual Goal

When accompanied by his peer mentor and given a digital map on a smartphone, Keej will independently use the city's rental scooter to transport himself between home and college with 100% accuracy.

Benchmarks/Short-Term Objectives

a. By May, when accompanied by his peer mentor and given a digital map on a smartphone, Keej will independently use an electric scooter to transport himself from **home to college**, arriving safely and on time, with 100% accuracy, and he will maintain this skill when probed weekly for at least two months.

b. By October, when accompanied by his peer mentor and given a digital map on a smartphone, Keej will independently use an electric scooter to transport himself from **college to home**, arriving safely and on time, with 100% accuracy, and he will maintain this skill when probed weekly for at least two months.

FIGURE 8   Keej's Benchmarks Task Analyzed.

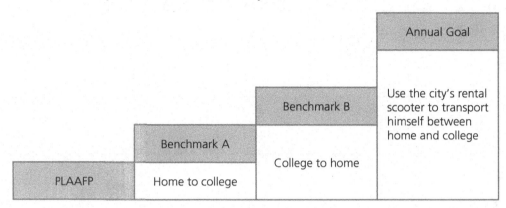

MAY I SEE EXAMPLES OF INCOMPLETELY WRITTEN BENCHMARKS?

Here are two examples:

1. Demetri will cook a frozen meal in a microwave oven without burning it.

YES **(NO)**   statement of conditions in which the behavior will be performed
(YES) NO   a statement of observable, measurable behavior
(YES) NO   a statement of criterion for mastery
YES **(NO)**   statement of generalization
YES **(NO)**   statement of maintenance

2. When Olivia's nose is runny and her teacher asks her to wipe it, Olivia will wipe her nose.

(YES) NO   a statement of conditions in which the behavior will be performed
(YES) NO   a statement of observable, measurable behavior
YES **(NO)**   statement of criterion for mastery
YES **(NO)**   statement of generalization
YES **(NO)**   statement of maintenance

TIME TO PRACTICE

Write two benchmarks for Benjamin's annual goal, using **each** of the given methods. When you finish, compare your answers with our suggestions in the appendix.

Annual Goal

When presented with 10 items and asked to count them, Benjamin will point to and orally count the items correctly with no prompts.

Performance

1. Benchmark _____

2. Benchmark _____

Assistance Level

1. Benchmark _____

2. Benchmark _____

Task Analysis

1. Benchmark _____

2. Benchmark _____

Generalization

1. Benchmark _____

2. Benchmark _____

SHORT-TERM OBJECTIVES

Short-term objectives describe multiple nonsequential yet related distinct skills necessary to achieve the annual goal. Short-term objectives are determined by listing the individual skills that must be mastered to accomplish the annual goal. Like benchmarks, short-term objectives describe the conditions, the behavior, and the criteria for mastery. They may also include statements for generalization and maintenance. See Figure 9.

FIGURE 9   Short-Term Objectives: Distinct Skills.

This example shows the "needs to" portion of a Present Levels of Academic Achievement and Functional Performance (PLAAFP) statement. The short-term objectives describe three non-sequential yet related distinct skills necessary to meet the annual goal.

PLAAFP "Needs to" Statement	Short-Term Objective 1	Short-Term Objective 2	Short-Term Objective 3	Annual Goal
Student needs to cover mouth when coughing or sneezing, rub lotion on dry skin, and put lip balm on dry lips.	Skill 1 Cover mouth/nose when coughing or sneezing.	Skill 2 Rub lotion on hands/arms.	Skill 3 Apply balm on dry or chapped lips.	Skills 1–3 Cover mouth/nose when coughing or sneezing, rub lotion, apply lip balm.

Let's look at a math example for Cadence.

Annual Goal

When assessed on the State Alternate Assessment at the end of the school year, Cadence will increase her math skills to a 1.6 grade level in at least 80% of the tested sub-domains (EE.2.MD.7; EE.1.OAA.1; EE.2.MD.8).

Short-term Objectives

a. When given a clock, Cadence will tell and write the time to the nearest five minutes, including a.m. and p.m., with at least 80% accuracy, with at least two different types of clocks (digital and analog), and she will maintain the skill when probed weekly for two weeks.

b. When given addition and subtraction problems within 20, Cadence will solve the problems with at least 80% accuracy, in two different settings (general and special education classrooms), and she will maintain this skill when probed weekly for two weeks.

c. When given simple word problems involving dollar bills, quarters, dimes, nickels, and pennies, Cadence will use $ and ¢ symbols with at least 80% accuracy, with various types of word problems, and she will maintain this skill when probed weekly for two weeks.

WE HAD BETTER PRACTICE THIS

Write two short-term objectives for Benjamin's annual goal. When you finish, check your answers with our suggestions with the appendix.

Annual Goal

When presented with 10 items and asked to count them, Benjamin will point to and orally count the items correctly with no prompts.

1. Short-term objective: _____

_____

_____

2. Short-term objective: _____

_____

_____

Let's summarize the elements of measurable annual goals, benchmarks, and short-term objectives.

1. Measurable annual goals describe the conditions, behavior, and criteria for achievement. They may also contain statements of generalization and maintenance.
2. Annual goals for students who take alternate assessments aligned to alternate achievement standards are broken down into benchmarks or short-term objectives.
3. Benchmarks break down annual goals into smaller sequential measurable parts and may include designated time intervals.
4. Short-term objectives break down annual goals into multiple related but distinct components without reference to specific time intervals.

 Excellent! You have practiced the second step for quality IEPs, so it's time to learn **Step 3**.

✔ Describe the student's present levels of academic achievement and functional performance.

✔ Write measurable annual goals.

STEP 3 Measure and report student progress.

STEP 4 State the services needed to achieve annual goals.

STEP 5 Explain the extent, if any, to which the student will not participate with nondisabled students in the regular class and in extracurricular and other nonacademic activities.

STEP 6 Explain accommodations necessary to measure academic achievement and functional performance on state and district-wide assessments.

STEP 7 Complete a transition plan for students ages 16 and older.

References

Endrew F. v. Douglas County School District Re-1, 580 U.S. 15-827 (2017).

Yates, J. (2014, April). *Exceeding the standard: A practical guide to developing and implementing IEP goals aligned with the common core state standards.* Paper presented at the Council for Exceptional Children Convention & Expo, Philadelphia, PA.

Measure and Report Student Progress

We have discussed the importance of writing appropriate annual goals in measurable terms so that the team agrees on the specific expectations for student improvement during the year. Why is measurement so important? Consider this parallel: If you make a New Year's resolution to lose 25 pounds by December but do not weigh yourself until October, you may not meet your goal. Regular monitoring of your weight enables you to watch your progress and determine whether you need to adjust your behavior. Similarly, regular measurement of student learning shows team members whether the student is making adequate progress. If progress is not measured, then the team cannot track the success of instruction, and the teacher cannot make necessary changes to help the student meet annual goals.

Parents are members of the IEP team, but they are not in school to observe their child's daily progress. Therefore, IDEA requires the team to include the following in the IEP:

- A description of **how** the student's progress toward meeting the annual goals will be measured
- A commitment to **when** periodic reports of the student's progress toward meeting the annual goals will be provided to the parents

Let's examine each of these.

WHAT ARE GOOD WAYS TO MEASURE PROGRESS TOWARD GOALS?

Measure progress by choosing the best way to monitor and record the observable behavior stated in the goal. For instance, fluency (speed and accuracy) in math facts is often measured by printed or digital timing sheets on which students either write or click on as many answers to printed facts as they can in one minute. The teacher then records the number of correct answers per minute and compares results to the goal criterion. Student work samples are common data sources, such as paragraphs written, color cards grouped, math problems correct, or science diagrams completed. Such informal curriculum-based measures are inexpensive, adaptable to specific skills, and easy to integrate into classroom learning activities.

Not all learning activities yield permanent student products, so teacher checklists are useful when measuring observable performance skills, such as counting to 20, following instructions for completing a science lab, or zipping a coat. The teacher simply records the date and whether the individual accomplished the task as described in the goal. Reading fluency is measured by having a student read a passage orally for one minute while an auditor marks errors on another copy and deducts them from the total words read to determine words read correctly per minute. Notice that Rajesh's IEP goal to identify story characters, setting, or plot requires that he *tell*. His teacher will record his performance on a checklist because telling does not produce a permanent product.

One high school teacher used this method as she helped students master a transition objective to check an automobile's engine oil. She first analyzed the steps to completing the task and then wrote them in sequential order, creating a task analysis. She then tested the task analysis with her paraeducator acting as a learner to make sure the steps would lead to the intended outcome. The teacher then assembled the students in the school parking lot to explain and model how to check the oil in a car. After sufficient guided practice she directed each student to independently complete a skill sequence including open the car hood, secure the hood, grasp the oil dipstick, extract it, state the oil level, replace the dipstick, replace the hood support, and close the hood. Her observation form listed each student's name and the eight components of the task. She entered the date for each component performed correctly by each student as her method to record progress toward the learning objective. Notice in the checklist below that Jazzi completed the sequence correctly on September 12, while Ben and Colly each omitted one step. This indicates that two students need further instruction and one or more additional opportunities to demonstrate mastery.

Objective: Complete oil check sequence independently

	Open hood	Support hood	Grasp dipstick	Extract dipstick	State oil level	Replace dipstick	Replace hood support	Close hood
Jazzi	9/12	9/12	9/12	9/12	9/12	9/12	9/12	9/12
Ben	9/12	9/12	9/12	9/12	9/12	9/12	9/12	—
Colly	9/12	9/12	9/12	9/12	—	9/12	9/12	9/12

Teachers also use observation checklists to record behavior data. Refer to Phoebe's IEP annual goal where she is to ask for help from a peer or adult at least one time for each assignment. Her teacher or other observer will record her behavior over time to determine if she is meeting the goal of asking for help 80% of opportunities to do so. Teachers use behavior observation and recording to monitor times out-of-seat, social skills such as saying "please" or listening politely, tardiness, or any other observable action. Behaviors are often measured in terms of frequency, latency, or duration, depending on the goal criterion. *Frequency* refers to how often the behavior occurs in a given time span. *Latency* refers to how long it takes for a behavior to occur after a teacher request or a triggering event. *Duration* measures the amount of time a behavior continues before stopping or changing.

Specific, descriptive data is essential for writing PLAAFP statements and for monitoring progress toward goal attainment. Using measurement and recording strategies that match goal behaviors and criteria makes student progress clear and understandable for all parties, including, of course, the students.

WHAT IF STUDENTS DO NOT ACHIEVE THEIR GOALS?

Do not fret; if students do not achieve their annual goals, you will not be prosecuted. The purpose of special education is to help students progress in the general curriculum or, in the case of some students with significant disabilities, in an appropriate alternate curriculum. IEP teams do their best to create goals that will help students progress, but no one can control what another person will achieve. Therefore, teachers and other team members must make their best efforts to help students achieve their goals and maintain records to show it. It is important to realize that unachieved goals are good data. If students do not progress, the teacher should adjust instruction and learning activities to improve learning. If the teacher has done everything possible to promote learning but the student is still unsuccessful, then teachers and team members seek to understand why and write more appropriate goals in the future.

HOW DO I DESCRIBE HOW PROGRESS WILL BE MEASURED?

You describe how progress will be measured by noting how data will be collected for each annual goal. You may begin by looking at the behavior and the criterion described in the goal and determining how that behavior can best be measured (e.g., percentage correct, number correct, rate, frequency, latency, or duration).

For example, Phoebe's second behavior goals states, "When presented with opportunities to interact with peers in small-group settings, Phoebe will initiate conversation and respond to maintain conversation 80% of opportunities as measured by adult observation." This means that the special education teacher, school psychologist, behavior specialist, or other trained observer will tally the number of times Phoebe initiates or responds to others to maintain conversation given the number of opportunities for her to do so. These tallies can then be converted to a percentage to determine progress toward the goal. When Phoebe achieves her goal 80% of opportunities over two weeks' time, she has achieved the goal.

You may recall that well-written annual goals address involvement and progress in the general curriculum and include criteria for achievement. The same types of assessment data used to create PLAAFP statements can be used to measure progress on goals. In Step 1 we described two general data sources:

1. Formal assessment (e.g., *Key Math, Kaufman Test of Educational Achievement, Vineland Adaptive Behavior Scales*)
2. Informal assessment (e.g., criterion-referenced tests, curriculum-based measures, work samples, student self-monitoring records, skill checklists, behavior checklists, home skill checklists)

The IEP must include the assessment used to measure progress, such as the name of a formal test, designation of a student work sample, plan for a teacher observation, or checklist for behavior.

LET'S SEE HOW THIS APPLIES TO IEPS FOR RAJESH, CADENCE, AND PHOEBE

Rajesh's Annual Goal

Given second-grade one- and two-syllable regularly and irregularly spelled words and weekly opportunities to practice, Rajesh will read the words correctly with at least 95% accuracy in one trial, as measured by teacher observation records (CCSS.ELA-LITERACY.RF2.3).

MEASUREMENT METHOD

The target behavior is to "read the words correctly with at least 95% accuracy in one trial." The measurement method is teacher observation records.

- Spoken answers can be recorded by the teacher on an observation checklist.

RATIONALE

The IEP team chose teacher observation because the teacher will listen to Rajesh read and mark errors. The number of words read correctly can then be converted to a percent of accuracy.

Cadence's Benchmark

When Cadence is asked to brush her hair, she will correctly find her brush and use it to detangle the left and right side of her hair, and the back within four minutes, 4/5 times without prompting, using various hair instruments, and she will maintain this skill when probed weekly for two consecutive weeks.

MEASUREMENT METHOD

The measurement method is a task analysis checklist completed by the teacher during each skill probe.

RATIONALE

The team chose a checklist as a simple method to track Cadence's accomplishment of each step in brushing her hair. The checklist with the date allows the teacher to determine when Cadence has met the criterion for each step within the task and when she has maintained the skill sufficiently to no longer be formally tracked.

Phoebe's Annual Goal for Behavior

Given a new or challenging assignment and without a teacher prompt, Phoebe will ask for help from a peer or adult at least one time for each assignment, 80% of opportunities over three weeks as measured by adult observation.

MEASUREMENT METHOD

The measurement method is teacher observation. Each time the teacher gives a new assignment she will mark if Phoebe asks a peer or adult for assistance. The number of occasions she asks for help divided by the total possible occasions multiplied by 100 will yield the percentage needed to monitor her goal achievement. For example, if Phoebe asks for assistance four out of a possible 13 times, she is asking 31% of opportunities, or less than half of the 80% criterion.

RATIONALE

The IEP team chose teacher observation because Phoebe is not likely to keep an accurate record herself, at least at first, and an informal behavior checklist provides the teacher with an easy tally system. The team needs the data, but wisely avoids burdening the classroom teacher with an unnecessarily complex and time-consuming measurement system—always a good idea for very busy colleagues.

TIME TO PRACTICE

Read each of the following goals and write two things:

1. An appropriate measurement method
2. Your rationale for choosing the method

Then check your answers with ours in the appendix.

Mikiah's Annual Goal

When presented with 20 items of clothing, Mikiah will sort the clothing to prepare for laundering with at least 80% accuracy once weekly for three consecutive weeks.

MEASUREMENT METHOD

☐ formal assessment ☐ criterion-referenced ☐ curriculum-based

☐ skills checklist ☐ behavior observation ☐ work sample

RATIONALE
(Why this method?): _____

_____

Alonzo's Annual Goal

When given a worksheet with 10 items of each type and directed by the teacher, Alonzo will add and subtract single-digit items and write answers with no errors.

MEASUREMENT METHOD

☐ formal assessment ☐ criterion-referenced ☐ curriculum-based

☐ skills checklist ☐ behavior observation ☐ work sample

RATIONALE

(Why this method?): _____

_____

WHAT ARE PROGRESS REPORTS FOR STUDENTS WITH IEPS?

Progress reports for students with disabilities are tools for school personnel to communicate with parents regarding their children's academic and functional progress toward meeting their IEP goals. School personnel may choose to send such reports in various ways—text messages, emails, letters, phone calls, and so forth. Schools usually require regular reports to be provided to parents and guardians of all students. The same standard applies for students with disabilities. But because they need specialized education and/or related services to make progress in the general curriculum, it is incumbent upon school personnel to provide specific details about these students' achievements. Schools and districts use a variety of reporting methods so you should check with your supervisors to determine the preferred method in your school.

HOW DO I DECIDE AND INDICATE WHEN PERIODIC REPORTS OF PROGRESS TOWARD ANNUAL GOALS WILL BE PROVIDED?

You must provide regular reports to parents regarding their children's progress, thus updating parents more often than at annual IEP meetings. IDEA requires that reports of IEP goal progress be issued at least as often as school report cards.

An IEP form might include a section for indicating when the reporting will be provided, such as the one shown here.

	Weekly	Biweekly	Monthly	Quarterly	Semiannually
Home note	X				
Progress report					
Parent conference					X
Report card				X	
Other					

HOW DOES THIS STEP IN THE IEP PROCESS IMPACT CLASSROOM PRACTICE?

Assessing and reporting each student's progress impacts classroom practice by requiring the teacher to do three things: measure, monitor, and report.

- *Measuring* is the act of administering some type of assessment to describe a student's academic or social behavior.
- *Monitoring* is the act of comparing student achievement to desired goals.
- *Reporting* provides oral or written information regarding student achievement.

Measuring

A teacher measures progress frequently to determine whether the students are progressing at the rate necessary to achieve their goals. Measures used are more frequently informal than formal, and the measurement schedule depends on the type of learning or behavior being assessed. The teacher may measure student progress several times a day, once a day, several times a week, once a week, or at some other appropriate interval.

Monitoring

A teacher monitors student progress by comparing measurement data with appropriate benchmarks. School-wide student progress is usually compared to state or district standards, grade-level or class progress is often monitored by comparison to groups of other students, and individual progress is compared to individual goals. Comparison with individual goals is the practice for students with IEPs. To determine if a student is making adequate progress toward IEP goals, a teacher must monitor frequently enough to either verify adequate progress or make necessary instructional changes to increase achievement.

Let's summarize how to measure and report student progress toward annual goals

The IEP must do the following:

1. Describe **how** the student's progress toward meeting the annual goals will be measured.
2. Describe **when** periodic reports of the progress the student is making toward meeting the annual goals will be provided.

Well done! You have studied and practiced Step 3. Now we will move to Step 4.

✔ Describe the student's present levels of academic achievement and functional performance.

✔ Write measurable annual goals.

✔ Measure and report student progress.

STEP 4 State the services needed to achieve annual goals.

STEP 5 Explain the extent, if any, to which the student will not participate with nondisabled students in the regular class and in extracurricular and other nonacademic activities.

STEP 6 Explain accommodations necessary to measure academic achievement and functional performance on state and district-wide assessments.

STEP 7 Complete a transition plan for students aged 16 and older.

State the Services Needed to Achieve Annual Goals

The statement of special education and related services on the IEP describes how and where specialized instruction will be provided to help students achieve their annual goals. You will remember that PLAAFP statements describe what the student is achieving at the time of the IEP and the annual goals describe what the student should achieve in one year.

MY MENTOR You can think of special education and related services as the bridge between achievement now and achievement in a year's time.

The IEP team begins by reviewing the student's current achievements, as noted in the PLAAFP statements, and considering the student's annual goals in order to determine which services will be required to meet them. This review is an important evaluative process enabling team members to make collaborative decisions for the student's education based on empirical evidence. Once services have been determined, the team decides how the services will be provided.

Unfortunately, some teams make these decisions in reverse order. They decide where the student should be served and what services will be provided—then they write the annual goals and PLAAFP statements. Quality IEPs that are legally correct are developed with the student's goals driving services and placement.

Special education and related services accomplish two purposes: (1) They help the student achieve annual goals, and (2) they do this in the *least restrictive environment*. Our discussion of special education and related services requires you to understand the least restrictive environment, so we define this term now.

WHAT IS THE LEAST RESTRICTIVE ENVIRONMENT?

IDEA requires that students with disabilities be educated in the least restrictive environment (LRE), which means educated with students without disabilities to the maximum extent appropriate, as determined by the IEP team. *Restrictive* in this case means any situation in which students with disabilities are served in special classes or separate schools or have otherwise been removed from the general class. Removing a student from the general classroom is appropriate when the IEP team determines that the nature or severity of the student's disability prevents satisfactory learning, even with supplementary aids or services provided.

The purpose of LRE is to ensure that students with disabilities spend as much time as feasible learning in the company of their peers without disabilities; to ensure that they are included in classroom activities and make progress in the general curriculum. This provision is designed to avoid the segregation so common in special education prior to IDEA in which students with disabilities had little or no contact with other students, often not even entering the school building, as in the case of Judy Heumann.

HOW DOES THE TEAM DETERMINE LEAST RESTRICTIVE ENVIRONMENT?

Determining LRE requires careful collaboration between team members and the student's various classroom teachers. The annual goals are the reference points. After the team creates appropriate goals, they then discuss what special education, related services, and/or supplementary aids and services will most likely help students achieve the goals, as described below. To better understand, let's look at Rajesh's first reading goal:

> Given second-grade one- and two-syllable regularly and irregularly spelled words and weekly opportunities to practice, Rajesh will read the words correctly with at least 95% accuracy, as measured by teacher observation records (CCSS.ELA-LITERACY.RF2.3).

For Rajesh, the grade-level team leader initiated the discussion by asking the others about services that will best help Rajesh meet this goal. The classroom teacher said that her data indicate that Rajesh will need intensive small-group or individual instruction. The resource teacher agreed, noting that the second-grade teacher has 29 students with a range of reading skills from moderately low to above grade level and no adult assistance. The school psychologist explained that Rajesh's reading skills are significantly lower than any other student in the classroom. His mother asked if the school has something in place to address this type of need. The LEA representative explained that the school does not have a multi-tiered system of supports in place to address Tier 2 or Tier 3 student needs. With further input from his mother, the team members decided that the least restrictive environment for Rajesh will be with the resource teacher in a separate classroom for 45 minutes each day. The team leader summarized this decision and asked if all agreed. They did, so this service pattern was recorded on his IEP.

Now let's look at Phoebe's goal to ask for help with assignments:

> Given a new or challenging assignment and without a teacher prompt, Phoebe will ask for help from a peer or adult at least one time for each assignment, 80% of opportunities as measured by adult observation over four weeks.

Phoebe's goal is designed to help her in the general classroom, so that is where her IEP team decides she will stay. However, her IEP indicates that she will work with the school psychologist as a related service provider for 30 minutes two times per week to address her anxiety and work on asking for assistance. This can be in the school psychologist's office or in the classroom, depending on Phoebe's progress, with the end goal to master the skill in the general classroom.

WHAT IS THE CONTINUUM OF PLACEMENTS AVAILABLE FOR STUDENTS WITH DISABILITIES?

If the IEP team determines that a student's needs cannot be met in the regular classroom, then the team members look at the continuum of placements that are more likely to meet the student's needs. This continuum moves from least to most restrictive and usually includes the following:

- Full inclusion in regular classes
- Less than half of each day in a resource classroom
- More than half of each day in a resource classroom
- Instruction in a self-contained classroom within the school
- Instruction in a separate school
- Instruction in the child's home
- Instruction in a hospital or institution

A student in any educational location can receive special education services. The services provided and the locations where they are delivered are determined by the IEP team within the requirements for LRE.

 It is important to understand that special education refers to services, **not** to a certain place in a building.

ARE THERE OTHER CONSIDERATIONS WHEN DETERMINING APPROPRIATE PLACEMENTS?

Yes. IDEA requires IEP teams to ensure that the student's educational placement is

- determined at least annually,
- based on the student's IEP, and
- provided as close as possible to the student's home.

This means the student is educated in the school he or she would attend if the student did not have a disability unless the team makes another selection with which the parent agrees. Some districts cluster students with significant disabilities in specialized classrooms in certain schools. While one IEP team might determine it is most appropriate for a student to be served in a school other than the one closest to home, another IEP team may determine the neighborhood school without a group of students with similar disabilities is the most appropriate.

In addition, when selecting the LRE, the team must consider any potential harmful effects on the child or on the quality of services needed. The student should not be removed from an age-appropriate regular class solely because of needed modifications in the general education curriculum. This means that when the student's needs can be met in the regular class by modifying the curriculum or providing supplemental aids or services, the student should not be removed to a more restrictive environment.

MY MENTOR   That's LRE. Now let's discuss services to help students with disabilities achieve their annual goals.

WHAT SERVICES ARE DESCRIBED ON THE IEP?

The law requires that the IEP state the services to be provided *to the student* or *on behalf of the student* and also specify the program modifications or supports provided for *school personnel* to help the student. IDEA requires that services be based on peer-reviewed research to the extent practicable. This means that the strategies, methods, and materials used to provide specially designed instruction should be well grounded in empirical research that substantiates effectiveness. You understand how important this is if you have noticed the cycle of unproven instructional fads and trendy practices that come and go in education.

Services provided to or on behalf of the student include

- special education services,
- related services, and
- supplementary aids and services.

Services provided for school personnel include

- program modifications and
- supports for teachers and related service providers.

All of the provided services must help the student

- advance appropriately toward attaining the annual goals,
- engage and make progress in the general education curriculum,
- participate in extracurricular and other nonacademic activities, and
- participate with peers both with and without disabilities in academic learning and additional activities.

Let's look at the services for students and school personnel.

WHAT ARE SPECIAL EDUCATION SERVICES?

Special education services refer to *specially designed instruction* to meet the unique needs of students with disabilities, as described in their annual goals. Specially designed instruction includes teaching, learning, practice, and assessment strategies that help students with disabilities achieve annual goals; this may involve adaptations to the general curriculum.

Who receives special education services?

Students whose annual IEP goals require specially designed instruction receive special education services. They are eligible for services only if they have been classified with a disability and have a current IEP. IDEA states that children with disabilities are those who experience developmental delays (ages 3–9) or are classified with one of the 12 disabilities.

Who provides special education services?

Special education services are provided by or under the direction of licensed special educators. Special education paraeducators may also provide services to students with disabilities, but they must do so under the direction of a licensed special educator.

How do I write special education services on the IEP?

Here is an example of special education services for Rajesh:

Special Education and Related Services

R = *Regular class*   S = *Special class*   O = *Other*   D = *Daily*   W = *Weekly*   M = *Monthly*

Service	Location	Time	Frequency	Begin date	Duration
Specially designed instruction for reading	R S̲ O	45 min	D̲ W M	10/22	1 yr

The IEP team has decided that the special education teacher will need to provide specially designed reading instruction for Rajesh. This will occur in the resource room for 45 minutes each day.

WHAT ARE RELATED SERVICES?

Related services refer to transportation, as well as developmental, corrective, and other supportive services needed to help a student with disabilities benefit from special education. The following services are options:

- Counseling, including rehabilitation counseling
- Early identification and assessment of disabling conditions
- Interpreting services

- Medical services
- Orientation and mobility services
- Physical and occupational therapy
- Psychological services
- Recreation, including therapeutic recreation
- School nurse services
- Social work services
- Speech-language pathology and audiology services
- Transportation

Who receives related services?

Any student with an IEP may receive related services that are necessary for the student to benefit from special education, as decided by the IEP team. For example, a student may receive specialized instruction for specific learning disabilities and also receive speech-language services. Another student may require orientation and mobility services but not receive any other specially designed instruction.

Who provides related services?

Each related service is provided by or under the direction of the professional who is licensed to provide it. IEP teams commonly include a school psychologist, a speech-language pathologist, a physical therapist, or an occupational therapist, depending on students' needs.

Where are related services provided?

As noted earlier, multidisciplinary teams decide the least restrictive environment for each child with an IEP. Related services can be provided in a regular classroom, in a separate room or office, or in an extracurricular setting, depending on student needs to be educated in the least restrictive environment.

How do I write related services on the IEP?

Here are the related services added to Phoebe's IEP:

Special Education and Related Services

R = Regular class   S = Special class   O = Other   D = Daily   W = Weekly   M = Monthly

Service	Location	Time	Frequency	Begin date	Duration
Behavior intervention	<u>R</u> S O: R S <u>O</u>: School psychologist office	5 hrs. 60 min	<u>D</u> W M D <u>W</u> M	1/22 1/22	1 yr 1 yr

You will notice that Phoebe's IEP specifies school psychology services to address her goals to improve behavior. The school psychologist will teach Phoebe replacement behaviors to encourage engagement and conversation with others in class. However, this level of detail is not required on the IEP; the team only needs to note that Phoebe will receive behavior services provided by the school psychologist.

WHAT ARE SUPPLEMENTARY AIDS AND SERVICES?

Supplementary aids and services refer to aids, services, and other supports provided in regular education classes or other education-related settings to enable students with disabilities to be educated with nondisabled students to the maximum extent appropriate (notice the emphasis on LRE). These services are provided when the IEP team determines that the student will need adjustments or modifications to the general curriculum or additional instruction in order to meet IEP goals.

When supplementary aids and services are needed, the IEP team may determine that teachers must make adjustments or modifications in one or more of the following areas:

1. The ways teachers present information:
   - A student with visual impairments may need large-print materials.
   - A student who is deaf and lip reads may need to see the teacher's face when he is speaking.
   - A student who cannot process sequential instructions may need the teacher to model each of the steps and provide a step-by-step list to follow.
2. The ways students complete tasks:
   - A student who has poor motor skills may need to dictate written expression to a scribe.
   - A student who has difficulty grasping math concepts may need instruction with manipulative objects to learn new skills or concepts.
   - A student may require assistive technology for speaking, listening, reading, or writing.
3. The ways teachers assess student learning:
   - A student who processes information slowly may need additional time to complete a test.
   - A student who attends school only in the afternoon due to a health impairment will need tests scheduled for afternoon.
   - A student who is highly distractible may need to be tested in a distraction-free environment.
   - A student who has a visual impairment or reading difficulty may need to have a test dictated.
   - A student who cannot speak may need to point to indicate answers to test items.
4. The ways teachers structure the environment:
   - A student who is easily distracted may need reduced-distraction seating or work areas, away from windows, fish tanks, open doors, or other areas with heavy traffic or sensory stimuli.

- A student using a walker will need wide enough pathways to access all areas of the classroom.
- A student who uses a wheelchair will need materials and equipment placed within reach.
- A student with visual impairments will need a stable, predictable physical environment in which change is rare in order to navigate easily in the classroom.
- A student who has a hearing impairment will need visual access to any information that other students learn by hearing, such as the public address system or movies/videos shown in class.
- A student who has difficulty learning and following classroom routines may benefit from a posted daily schedule to anticipate transitions between activities.

Who receives supplementary aids and services?

Any student with an IEP may receive supplementary aids and services if the services are necessary for the student to benefit from special education. For example, a student who cannot use a regular computer keyboard may need an adapted keyboard with larger keys. Another student may require large-print materials but not require specially designed instruction.

Who provides supplementary aids and services?

Supplementary aids and services may be provided by a regular class teacher, paraeducator, special educator, related service provider, or other qualified school personnel. For example, the school administrator may purchase equipment or provide alterations to the school facilities if required.

Where are supplementary aids and services provided?

Supplementary aids and services are provided in the regular class or in other curricular or extracurricular environments to meet the student's IEP goals. The primary focus of providing supplementary aids and services is to facilitate student success in the regular class and in other environments with nondisabled peers.

How do I write supplementary aids and services on the IEP?

Let's look at an example. Here is the supplementary aids and services statement from Cadence's IEP:

Program Modifications and/or Supplementary Aids and Services in Regular Classes

Supplementary Aids and Services	Frequency
Paraeducator in general classroom 4 hrs.	<u>D</u> W M

Cadence's regular class teacher has never taught a child with Down syndrome, so the team has determined that a paraeducator should be in the classroom daily to support the teacher's instruction and facilitate student learning for Cadence and other students who need assistance.

WHAT ARE PROGRAM MODIFICATIONS OR SUPPORTS?

Program modifications or supports assist teachers to meet unique and specific needs of students with disabilities. Let's briefly explore these terms:

- *Program modifications* include interventions and accommodations necessary for the teacher to help the student achieve IEP goals. For example, a student whose behavior interferes with learning will need a program of positive behavioral supports to learn more appropriate and productive behaviors. The IEP team would discuss these unique and specific needs, describe the necessary modifications on the IEP, and provide the support the teacher needs to implement the program.
- *Supports* include special training for teachers to help them meet unique or specific needs of students in the classroom. For example, a teacher may need to learn how to enter new vocabulary words into a student's communication device so the student can use the vocabulary as other students are assigned to do. Supports for teachers might also include having a paraeducator in the classroom or acquiring technology such as that highlights key words in a multimedia presentation.

Who receives program modifications or supports?

School personnel who are responsible for addressing a student's goals receive program modifications or supports, which are noted on the IEP.

Who provides program modifications or supports?

School personnel may receive program modifications or supports from a special educator, a paraeducator, a related service provider, a staff developer or another education professional.

Where are program modifications or supports provided?

Program modifications or supports can be provided in the regular classroom or in other curricular or extracurricular environments to meet the student's IEP goals. These modifications and supports should help the student achieve annual goals in the least restrictive environment.

How do I write program modifications or supports on the IEP?

Phoebe's IEP includes this program support for her teachers:

Program Modifications and/or Supplementary Aids and Services in Regular Classes

Modifications/Personnel Support	Frequency	Supplementary Aids and Services	Frequency
School psychologist will consult with general education teacher to teach and model behavior data collection and positive reinforcement in the classroom.	D W M <u>O</u>: *Initial training, and follow-up as needed.*		D W M

Phoebe has behavior change goals, so the school psychologist's support will help her general classroom teacher implement the behavior plan.

WHAT SPECIAL FACTORS DOES THE TEAM CONSIDER?

Depending on the needs of the student, the IEP team must consider what IDEA calls *special factors*, as noted below:

- If the student's behavior interferes with his or her learning or the learning of others, the IEP team will consider positive behavior interventions and supports to address the problems.
- If the student has limited proficiency in English, the IEP team will consider the student's language needs as they relate to his or her IEP.
- If the student is blind or visually impaired, the IEP team must provide for using and instructing in Braille, unless they determine after an appropriate evaluation that the student does not need this instruction.
- If the student is deaf or hard of hearing or has other language or communication needs, the IEP team must consider those needs. This includes enabling the student to communicate directly with classmates and school staff in his or her usual method of communication (e.g., sign language).
- The IEP team must consider the student's need for assistive technology devices or services.

Here is one way special factors can be indicated on an IEP:

Applicable Special Factors

Factor	Not Needed	In IEP
Positive behavior instruction and support when behavior impedes learning of student or others		✔
Language needs for student with limited English proficiency	✔	

Factor	Not Needed	In IEP
Braille instruction for student who is blind or visually impaired	✔	
Communication and/or language services for student who is deaf or hard of hearing or has other communication needs		✔
Assistive technology devices or services		✔

You can also refer to Cadence's IEP. It indicates that she needs communication and/or language services.

HOW DOES THE TEAM DECIDE WHAT SERVICES THE STUDENT NEEDS?

The team considers the student's PLAAFP statements and annual goals and then decides the types of service that will best help the student achieve the goals. For example, if you look at Keej's IEP, you will see that he has annual goals in math, language arts, social/emotional, communication, functional life skills, and career/vocational. You will also note that the IEP team determined that a range of services for Keej are necessary to achieve the goals.

MAY I SEE EXAMPLES OF IEP TEAM DECISIONS FOR DETERMINING SERVICES?

Sure. Refer to the IEPs for the four students who have served as examples throughout these instructions. You will see the services listed after the annual goals. This IEP format is a good reminder that teams first establish annual goals, and then decide which services are needed to meet those goals.

LET'S PRACTICE

Refer to Cadence's IEP and answer the following questions. Then compare your answers with the appendix.

1. What special education services does Cadence require?

2. What related services does Cadence require?

3. What supplementary aids and services does Cadence require?

4. What program modifications and supports do Cadence's teachers require?

5. What special factors did the IEP team consider?

6. Explain why you think the team recommended these services.

WHAT DECISIONS DOES THE TEAM MAKE REGARDING THE DATE, FREQUENCY, LOCATION, AND DURATION OF SERVICES TO BE PROVIDED?

Once the team decides which special education and related services are required, they record this information on the IEP and then specify the following:

- **Date.** The IEP should designate when the special education and related services will begin. The IEP is in effect when it is signed by the team, but services might not begin until the next school day.
- **Frequency.** The IEP should also indicate how often the services will be provided. The decision about frequency of services is made by the team and agreed on by those who provide the services.

 Check with your school or district to find out whether time increments are to be recorded in minutes or hours by the day, week, or month.

- **Location.** Location for the services should also be included. Remember, the team is required by IDEA to provide services in the least restrictive environment.
- **Duration.** The team must also decide and record the length of time the services will be provided. IDEA requires the team to review the IEP at least annually, but the team may review and/or rewrite the IEP more often if needed to meet the individual needs of the student.

These important aspects of the IEP provide specific information to parents, teachers, and students regarding the number and type of services the student will receive and when and where those services will be provided. The IEP form or program will have a place to specify this information, perhaps similar to the examples above.

IS THERE ANYTHING TRICKY TO WATCH FOR AT THIS STAGE OF IEP DEVELOPMENT?

Yes, there is. A common error occurs when the team confuses the term *service* with the term *location*. For example, it is incorrect for the team to write "special class" as a service; "special class" is a *location*. The type of service would be specially designed instruction, speech therapy, life skills instruction, or some other such designation.

ARE THERE SPECIAL CONSIDERATIONS FOR PROVIDING SERVICES TO SECONDARY STUDENTS WITH IEPS?

Yes. IDEA requires that IEP teams address transition planning for students age 16 and older. You will learn this important process in Step 7.

Let's summarize the requirements for Step 4

1. Determine which services will be provided *to* or *on behalf of* the student, which may include
   - special education services,
   - related services, and
   - supplementary aids and services.
2. Determine which services will be provided for *school personnel*, which may include
   - program modifications and
   - supports.
3. Make sure that all of the provided services will help the student
   - advance appropriately toward attaining the annual goals,
   - engage and make progress in the general education curriculum,
   - participate in extracurricular and other nonacademic activities, and
   - participate with peers both with and without disabilities in academic learning and additional activities.

Whew! You've completed Step 4, so let's see what happens in **Step 5**.

   ✔   Describe the student's present levels of academic achievement and functional performance.

   ✔   Write measurable annual goals.

   ✔   Measure and report student progress.

   ✔   State the services needed to achieve annual goals.

STEP 5   Explain the extent, if any, to which the student will not participate with nondisabled students in the regular class and in extracurricular and other nonacademic activities.

STEP 6   Explain accommodations necessary to measure academic achievement and functional performance on state- and district-wide assessments.

STEP 7   Complete a transition plan for students aged 16 and older.

Explain the Extent, if Any, to Which the Student Will Not Participate with Nondisabled Students in the Regular Class and in Extracurricular and Other Nonacademic Activities

The law, through the LRE requirement, assumes that every student with disabilities will be involved and progress in the general education curriculum. All students with disabilities will also participate with nondisabled students in regular classes, as well as in extracurricular and other nonacademic activities. When a student is not to participate, the IEP team must determine why such participation is not appropriate and include a statement of the extent to which the student will not participate.

WHAT ARE THE CONCERNS ABOUT EXCLUDING STUDENTS WITH DISABILITIES FROM REGULAR CLASSES AND ACTIVITIES?

Concerns about excluding students from any aspect of the regular school program are related to the effects of exclusion. When students do not participate in regular classroom activities, they do not benefit from teachers' content knowledge and from opportunities to learn with and from their peers without disabilities. And when students are restricted from extracurricular or other nonacademic activities, they miss important social interactions and opportunities to enrich their life experiences in the same ways as students without disabilities.

 Remember, the spirit and intent of LRE are to make sure all students have access to the general curriculum to the maximum extent appropriate.

WHAT IS MEANT BY THE TERMS *REGULAR CLASS*, *EXTRACURRICULAR ACTIVITIES*, AND *OTHER NONACADEMIC ACTIVITIES*?

These terms should not be confused with the general curriculum. The general curriculum can be taught in a separate special education setting, but students would be excluded from participating with their peers without disabilities. The following examples will help you understand what is meant by these terms.

The general class

Typically, the general class is where students with disabilities receive instruction in the general curriculum with nondisabled peers. This is the designation for grade-level classes in elementary schools and for required or elective classes in secondary settings. It is also called the *general education class* or other similar names, depending on school district or state terminology.

Extracurricular activities

Extracurricular activities are supplementary to the general curriculum, not required by state curriculum standards. They generally vary from school to school and may include activities such as

- sports,
- peer leadership,
- Knowledge Bowl, and
- school clubs.

Nonacademic activities

Nonacademic activities are part of the school day, but they are not directly related to mandated curriculum or extracurricular activities. These may include

- breakfast,
- lunch,
- recess,
- school assemblies, and
- class parties.

HOW DOES THE IEP TEAM DETERMINE IF A STUDENT WILL NOT PARTICIPATE IN REGULAR CLASSES AND ACTIVITIES?

The team must make this determination by deciding whether the nature or severity of the disability would preclude satisfactory progress in the general curriculum even with the use of supplementary aids and services. For example, Martha is highly sensitive to noise and to crowds of people. Knowing that these sensitivities adversely affect her behavior and, thus, her progress in the curriculum, her team decided to exempt her from eating lunch in the cafeteria at the same time as other students and from participating in noisy, crowded classroom activities.

IEP teams must be cautious to avoid excluding a student from a regular school program based solely on disability classification. Most students who receive special education services can participate in the regular school program with varying degrees of adaptation or accommodation.

HOW DOES THE TEAM ADDRESS THIS DECISION ON THE IEP?

The IEP must include an explanation of the extent to which the student will not participate in the regular school program. You will need to learn what your district or state requires for this. The following example is from Cadence's IEP. This statement of nonparticipation is included under *Participation in Regular Class, Extracurricular, and Nonacademic Activities:*

> The student will participate in the regular class and in extracurricular and other nonacademic activities except as noted in special education and related services or listed here: *Cadence will not participate in math and language arts in the general education classroom 1–2 times per week so she can receive 1:1 instruction from the special education teacher.*

Cadence's IEP team realized that she needs some intensive instruction during the week to address her math and language arts goals. The special education teacher will provide the instruction in a separate setting during the general class math and language arts time, one to two times per week as needed.

YOUR TURN!

Read each of the following vignettes and write your advice for the IEP team regarding nonparticipation. When you are finished, compare your recommendations with those in the appendix.

> 1. Boston was born with cerebral palsy, which limits his fine and gross motor movement.
>
>   The student will participate in the regular class, extracurricular, and other nonacademic activities except as noted in special education and related services or listed here:
>
>   _____
>
>   _____

2. Asher receives specially designed behavior supports in all regular classes.

The student will participate in the regular class, extracurricular, and other nonacademic activities except as noted in special education and related services or listed here:

_____

_____

Let's summarize the extent of nonparticipation in the regular class and in extracurricular and other nonacademic activities.

1. Students with disabilities are expected to participate in regular classes and activities.
2. The three areas in which students with disabilities participate are
   • the regular class,
   • extracurricular activities, and
   • other nonacademic activities.
3. The IEP must include a statement explaining the extent to which a student will not participate in the regular class and/or in extracurricular and other nonacademic activities.
4. This statement can list specific classes or activities in which the student will not participate.

Well done! You have practiced the fifth step for writing quality IEPs, so it's time to learn **Step 6**.

✔   Describe the student's present levels of academic achievement and functional performance.

✔   Write measurable annual goals.

✔   Measure and report student progress.

✔   State the services needed to achieve annual goals.

✔   Explain the extent, if any, to which the student will not participate with nondisabled students in the regular class and in extracurricular and other nonacademic activities.

STEP 6   Explain accommodations necessary to measure academic achievement and functional performance on state- and district-wide assessments.

STEP 7   Complete a transition plan for students aged 16 and older.

Explain Accommodations Necessary to Measure Academic Achievement and Functional Performance on State- and District-Wide Assessments

Consistent with the goal of involvement and progress in the general education curriculum, students with disabilities are to participate with nondisabled students in state- and district-wide assessments. Their participation assures that education professionals are accountable for the appropriate progress of all students. The law requires the IEP team to include a statement of any individual accommodations that are necessary to measure a child's academic achievement and functional performance on state- and district-wide assessments. If the team determines that a student with disabilities cannot reasonably participate in all or part of one of these assessments even with accommodations, then the team must select an alternate assessment for that student.

HOW MIGHT STUDENTS WITH DISABILITIES PARTICIPATE IN STATE- OR DISTRICT-LEVEL ASSESSMENTS?

Students with disabilities can participate in state- or district-level assessments under any of several conditions, based on the IEP team's decision. You can see this in each of our case study student's IEPs. Not all states offer all assessment options, so you need to check your state regulations to learn which options are available. The following choices are generally offered:

- Regular assessment of grade-level academic content standards based on grade-level academic achievement standards
- Regular assessment of grade-level academic content standards with appropriate *accommodations*, based on grade-level academic achievement standards

- Alternate assessment of grade-level academic content standards based on grade-level academic achievement standards
- Alternate assessment of grade-level academic content standards based on *alternate* academic achievement standards, as explained in Step 1.

WHEN ARE STUDENTS WITH DISABILITIES ASSESSED ON STATE- AND DISTRICT-WIDE ASSESSMENTS?

Students with disabilities are tested on the same schedule as those without disabilities. Federal law requires systematic assessment of student progress in specified grades for certain subjects (e.g., language arts, math, or science); however, your state or school district might require additional tests. Be sure to check with your school or district regarding the scheduling of state- and district-wide assessments.

 MY MENTOR Now let's learn how to make IEP decisions for each of these options.

WHAT IS REGULAR ASSESSMENT OF GRADE-LEVEL ACADEMIC CONTENT STANDARDS BASED ON GRADE-LEVEL ACADEMIC ACHIEVEMENT STANDARDS?

This means students with disabilities take the same tests under the same conditions as students without disabilities.

How does the team decide that a student will participate in this option?

The IEP team may decide that a student with a disability who has performed at capacity on previous assessments will take the same tests under the same conditions as students without disabilities. This decision must be made with substantial evidence that taking the tests under standardized conditions does not prevent the student from demonstrating competency.

WHAT IS REGULAR ASSESSMENT OF GRADE-LEVEL ACADEMIC CONTENT STANDARDS WITH APPROPRIATE ACCOMMODATIONS BASED ON GRADE-LEVEL ACADEMIC ACHIEVEMENT STANDARDS?

This means that students with disabilities take the same tests as students without disabilities but under different conditions. The IEP team must remember that participating with accommodations means there are no changes to test content or administration that *fundamentally alter or lower the standard or expectations of the assessment.*

How does the team decide that a student will participate in this option?

The team should consider whether or not the student requires accommodations for classroom instruction and tests. If accommodations are required in the course of daily learning and classroom assessments, then the student will most likely require the same or similar accommodations for state- and district-wide assessments, depending on the content being assessed.

How does the team select appropriate accommodations for state- and district-wide assessments?

The team can select appropriate accommodations based on answers to these or similar questions:

- What accommodations does the student regularly use in the classroom and on tests of content similar to that covered on the state- or district-wide assessment?
- What is the student's perception of the efficacy of the accommodations regularly used? Has the student been willing to use the accommodations?
- What evidence is available from parents, teachers, or others about the efficacy of an accommodation?
- Have there been difficulties administering the selected accommodations?

While the difficulty of providing specific accommodations should not warrant dismissing them, IEP teams may select different accommodations that are equally effective but not as intrusive or difficult to administer.

What are some examples of assessment accommodations?

As we look at examples, please remember that accommodations do not fundamentally change the content or administration of the test in ways that alter or lower the standard or expectations of the assessment. Be sure to check your state or district guidelines to learn which accommodations are acceptable within this definition. Here are several examples of accommodations for various domains of test administration.

Setting

- Provide a distraction-free environment such as a study carrel
- Provide special furniture, such as an adjustable-height desk for a wheelchair
- Provide a small-group setting

Scheduling

- Provide extended testing time within the same day
- Administer the test in several sessions within total time allowance

Test format

- Provide a Braille edition
- Present the test in the student's native language if available
- Increase spacing, including fewer items per page or only one sentence per line
- Provide magnification or amplification equipment

Test directions

- Read directions to the student
- Provide recorded directions
- Simplify language in order to clarify or explain
- Repeat directions for subtasks

Test procedures

- Read content aloud, except for reading subtests in which specific skills being assessed preclude reading aloud
- Use sign language for orally presented test items
- Provide written copies of orally presented materials that are found only in the administrator's manual

Student response format

- Allow an adult to enter the student's answer on a web-based test
- Permit the student to answer by pointing, signing, typing, responding orally, or providing another non-written response
- Audio record the student's responses
- Provide a template or placeholder for the answer document

MAY I SEE AN EXAMPLE OF SELECTED ACCOMMODATIONS ON AN IEP?

Sure. Refer to Rajesh's IEP, and notice that his PLAAFP statement indicates that he does not read at the first-grade level. Under the section "Participation in State and District Assessment," the team noted that Rajesh should have the *test directions* read aloud in English for language arts and math and science, and that the math and science *test items* should be read aloud in English. The language arts test items would not be read aloud because doing so would fundamentally alter or lower the standard or expectations of the reading assessment.

Practice choosing appropriate accommodations for these students

Read each of the following cases and write your suggestions for appropriate accommodations for state- and district-wide assessments. You can refer to the examples above. Then compare your answers with our suggestions in the appendix.

1. Amara has fine motor limitations that prevent her from holding or using a pencil.
   Suggested accommodation: _____

   _____

2. Derrick has visual impairments that prevent him from reading print of normal size.
   Suggested accommodation: _____

   _____

3. Kalappan's attention deficit disorder significantly impairs his ability to concentrate in groups larger than three or four students.
   Suggested accommodation: _____

   _____

WHAT IS ALTERNATE ASSESSMENT OF GRADE-LEVEL ACADEMIC CONTENT STANDARDS BASED ON GRADE-LEVEL ACADEMIC ACHIEVEMENT STANDARDS?

This option addresses the same content and holds students to the same expectations as does the regular grade-level test, but students participate in some way other than the usual paper and pencil or computer-based test. For example, students may demonstrate content mastery through work samples aligned with the grade-level standards.

IEP teams must be cautious in selecting the alternate means by which students will demonstrate their skills because these alternate tests must be comparable to the regular assessments as well as valid and reliable in order to be eligible for determining the student's annual progress.

How does the team decide that a student will participate in a particular option?

Similar to determining appropriate accommodations, the team considers ways that the student successfully demonstrates learning in the classroom on comparable content. If sufficient evidence shows that the student more accurately demonstrates achievement or ability in an alternate way, then the IEP team may choose this option.

WHAT IS ALTERNATE ASSESSMENT OF GRADE-LEVEL ACADEMIC CONTENT STANDARDS BASED ON *ALTERNATE* ACADEMIC ACHIEVEMENT STANDARDS?

This option means students are tested on grade-level content but with altered expectations for performance. As the term indicates, modifications *modify* (alter) some aspect of the way the test is presented or the way the student responds to test items.

How does the team decide that a student will participate with this option?

As with accommodations, the team considers any modifications required for the student to be successful in daily learning. The student will most likely require the same or similar modifications for state- and district-wide assessments.

How does the team select appropriate modifications for state- and district-wide assessments?

As with accommodations, the team considers the modifications needed for the student to experience academic success in the classroom: whether the student prefers and uses these modifications, if the modifications have been effective, and whether other modifications might be less difficult to administer while obtaining similar results.

MAY I SEE SOME EXAMPLES OF ASSESSMENT MODIFICATIONS?

Certainly. Here are several examples of modifications for some domains of test administration:

Test format

- Highlight key words or phrases.
- Place visual cues on the test form, such as arrows or "stop" signs.
- Assist students by pointing.
- Reduce the number of test items.

Test procedures

- Audio record or read the entire test when it includes reading subtests.
- Sign or cue the test.
- Read aloud complex multiple step math questions one step at a time.
- Allow a calculator to be used for non-calculator tests or subtests.
- Allow use of manipulative math objects not provided to all students.

Student response format

- Allow reference materials not provided to all students (e.g., a multiplication table).
- Allow use of a spelling and/or grammar check for tests or subtests of spelling or composition.
- Provide a scribe for tests or subtests of writing.

Remember that modifications cause the content or administration of the test to be fundamentally changed in ways that alter or lower the standard or expectations of the assessment. If the test publisher does not allow certain changes to the test content or administration, those changes would be considered modifications.

 You will need to check test administration requirements to determine which changes are considered accommodations (not lowering the standard) or modifications (lowering the standard).

LET'S PRACTICE CHOOSING APPROPRIATE MODIFICATIONS

Read each of the following cases and write your suggestions for appropriate modifications for state- and district-wide assessments. Compare your answers with our suggestions in the appendix.

1. Duong's visual impairment prevents him from reading print on a reading test, but he has good listening comprehension skills.

   Suggested modification: _____

   _____

2. Novia has a health impairment that significantly reduces the amount of time she can work without resting.

   Suggested modification: _____

   _____

WHAT IS ALTERNATE ASSESSMENT ALIGNED WITH GRADE-LEVEL ACADEMIC CONTENT STANDARDS SCORED AGAINST ALTERNATE ACADEMIC ACHIEVEMENT STANDARDS?

As described in Step 1, this alternate assessment is based on alternate achievement standards that are linked to grade-level content standards but have been reduced in complexity, depth, or breadth. These tests reflect an alternate level of expectations compared to regular assessments or alternate assessments based on grade-level achievement standards. In general, alternate achievement standards must

- be aligned with a state's academic content standard,
- promote access to the general curriculum, and
- reflect professional judgment of the highest achievement standards possible.

MY MENTOR Step 1 explains that the *Every Student Succeeds Act* restricts this testing to no more than **1% of students** in a state or district.

How does the team decide that a student will participate in this option?

The team decides by considering established guidelines for having a student participate in this type of testing rather than in the standard state- or district-wide assessment. This option applies to students who

- have the most significant cognitive disabilities and do not reach grade-level academic standards, even with appropriate instruction, and/or
- participate in a curriculum more closely aligned with an alternate curriculum rather than the general curriculum.

What must be included on the IEP if a student takes an alternate assessment?

IEP teams are given authority to administer alternate assessments appropriate for measuring students' academic achievement and functional performance. However, the types of assessments from which these teams can choose depend on individual state or district regulations. Generally, the types of assessments available include checklists, portfolios, and task performance demonstrations, including the use of assistive technology. These assessments must have an explicit structure as well as clearly delineated scoring criteria and procedures. They also should be valid, reliable, accessible, objective, and consistent with nationally recognized professional and technical standards.

The IEP must include a statement explaining

- why the student cannot participate in the regular assessment, and
- why the particular alternate assessment selected is appropriate for the student.

MY MENTOR Be sure to check with your school district regarding alternate assessment options in your state.

MAY I SEE AN EXAMPLE OF THIS KIND OF STATEMENT?

Of course. Take a look at Cadence's IEP and you will see the following statements:

Alternate Assessment:

State why student cannot participate in regular assessment.

Cadence's skills in math and language arts are approximately two years behind her typically developing peers; her poor communication skills and limited attention span impair her ability to successfully demonstrate achievement on standardized tests.

State why selected alternate assessment is appropriate.

Cadence was administered the State Alternate Assessment at the beginning of this year and was able to demonstrate her skills, given multiple testing breaks, prompts to stay on task, concrete examples, and multiple explanations of the tasks, in a 1:1 setting.

LET'S PRACTICE CHOOSING APPROPRIATE ALTERNATE ASSESSMENTS

Read each of the following cases and mark your suggestions for either standard assessment or alternate assessment. Compare your answers with ours in the appendix.

1. Ezzie requires substantial adaptations and supports to meaningfully access the grade-level content, requires intensive individualized instruction to acquire and generalize knowledge, and is unable to demonstrate achievement of academic content standards on a paper and pencil test, even with accommodations.

    ☐ Standard assessment   ☐ Alternate assessment

2. Aisha's significant cognitive disability and orthopedic impairments prevent her from successfully participating in standardized assessments, even with accommodations and modifications.

    ☐ Standard assessment   ☐ Alternate assessment

Let's summarize how the team explains necessary accommodations for state- and district-wide assessments

The team considers the student's strengths, needs, and abilities, and then chooses one of these options, as allowed by the particular state, and plans accordingly:

- Regular assessment of grade-level academic content standards based on grade-level academic achievement standards
- Regular assessment of grade-level academic content standards with appropriate *accommodations,* based on grade-level academic achievement standards
- Alternate assessment of grade-level academic content standards based on grade-level academic achievement standards
- Alternate assessment of grade-level academic content standards based on *alternate* academic achievement standards

MY MENTOR | One more step to consider. The team must complete a **transition plan** for students aged 16 and older.

✔   Describe the student's present levels of academic achievement and functional performance.

✔   Write measurable annual goals.

✔   Measure and report student progress.

✔   State the services needed to achieve annual goals.

✔   Explain the extent, if any, to which the student will not participate with nondisabled students in the regular class and in extracurricular and other nonacademic activities.

✔   Explain accommodations necessary to measure academic achievement and functional performance on state- and district-wide assessments.

STEP 7   Complete a transition plan for students aged 16 and older.

Complete a Transition Plan for Students Aged 16 and Older

Transition planning is a student-centered process of structuring coursework and other educational experiences to prepare the student for transition from school to adult life. Transition planning is based on assessment and results in a formal document that is individualized to the needs and aspirations of the student for adult living.

IDEA requires that the IEP team develop a transition plan beginning with the IEP in effect when the student turns 16, or younger if determined appropriate by the IEP team. Some states set the mandatory age at 14. Transition plans must be reviewed and updated annually until the student either reaches age 22 or no longer requires special education services. Students with disabilities who graduate with a diploma or who receive a certificate of completion are no longer eligible for special education services according to IDEA. Therefore, it is incumbent upon the team to determine what goals and services are most appropriate for students in order to facilitate a smooth transition to post-secondary activities.

WHO IS INVOLVED IN TRANSITION PLANNING?

The student is central to successful transition planning regardless of academic achievement or functional performance. The IEP team works with the student and parents or guardians to create the IEP and the transition plan. Transition usually involves community-based services such as vocational rehabilitation, post-secondary education and training, college accessibility programs, mental health services, employers, and/or others, so representatives of these entities serve on the team as applicable.

DOES TRANSITION PLANNING EVER APPLY TO STUDENTS YOUNGER THAN 16?

Yes. The IEP team may begin transition planning and services at an earlier age if the effects of the student's disability are such that more time is required to prepare for transition to adult life.

HOW DOES THE TEAM ACCOMPLISH TRANSITION PLANNING?

The first step in transition planning is for the student, in conjunction with the IEP team, to explore the student's aspirations for the future. IDEA requires that goals be "based upon age appropriate transition assessments related to training, education, employment, and where appropriate, independent living skills" (§300.43(a)(1)). As in any effective planning for students with disabilities, assessment is both a starting point and an ongoing process. Assessment for transition can use a range of formal and informal measures to determine a student's interests and needs regarding future academic pursuits, employment, daily living, social activity, and personal development. The student and IEP team use this information to create a transition plan and IEP goals detailing the academic, prevocational, social, and daily living experiences to be provided to prepare for life after school. Teams often use the National Secondary Transition Technical Assistance Center's checklists to help them meet minimum requirements in developing transition plans for students with disabilities (see the Transition Resources section at the end of Step 7).

WHAT TYPES OF ASSESSMENT SHOULD THE TEAM USE?

The team can use formal assessment, informal assessment, or a combination of both. Assessment is a recurring process to help the team stay current with the student's evolving skills, interests, and goals for the future. Assessment should help determine the student's sense of self, talents and interests, and life goals during school and for the future. The process should also identify potential barriers and options for overcoming them. We explain formal and informal assessment below.

Formal assessments

Formal transition assessments are norm-referenced or criterion-referenced and have standardized administration procedures, similar to standardized cognitive and academic tests. Some formal assessments are print-based and some are offered online or as commercial software tools. These assessments usually employ self-reported measures of interests, skills, and talents and provide results-based guidance to address academic needs in school as well as experiences for vocational, recreational, and daily living needs, like accessing community services, health care, public transportation, housing, and shopping.

Please anticipate potential problems with formal assessments related to a student's age, developmental level, reading ability, primary language, preferred form of communication, and culture. It is best to prepare yourself with training provided by test manuals or with face-to-face or online courses offered by test developers to insure appropriate administration and interpretation of test results.

Informal assessments

Informal assessments are inexpensive and often created by teachers to focus on person-specific skills or behaviors that formal assessments do not. There are several informal ways to collect information for transition planning, including school and parent records, interviews, questionnaires, and behavioral observations. Reviewing school records and parent reflections on school experiences can indicate strengths and difficulties with skills or courses. Interviewing a student using structured questions and follow-up probes to elicit additional details allows a team member to assess specific interests or concerns. A questionnaire can be a useful alternative to an oral interview by which the student chooses from a list of responses to each item or completes short-answer items. Finally, observing students over time in various situations and environments can indicate strengths or needs based on behavior. For example, observing a student requesting assistance from office personnel can indicate the student's level of comfort in asking for help. Please see the *Transition Resources* section at the end of Step 7 for a list of helpful information sources for formal and informal transition assessment and planning.

Assessment for transition will only be useful if it elicits practical information and if the team interprets and uses the data appropriately. The IEP team, student, and parent can then plan together to create a meaningful transition plan. We discuss this in detail below.

WHAT ARE THE REQUIREMENTS FOR A TRANSITION PLAN?

The transition plan must include these three components:

- Appropriate measurable **post-secondary goals** based upon age-appropriate transition assessments related to
  — training,
  — education,
  — employment,
  — and, where appropriate, independent living skills
- **Transition services**, including courses of study, necessary to assist the student in reaching the goals
- A statement that the student has been informed of **transfer of adult rights** not later than one year before the student reaches the age of majority

HOW DOES THE TEAM ACCOMPLISH TRANSITION PLANNING?

Let's answer this question by explaining how the team addresses each of the three elements: post-secondary goals, transition services, and transfer of adult rights.

MEASURABLE SECONDARY SCHOOL AND POST-SECONDARY GOALS

The law requires the goals to be based on data from appropriate transition assessments. This is best accomplished when the IEP team and representatives of community agencies that provide transition services use assessment results to guide discussions of the student's career interests, desires for continuing education, and expectations for independent adult living. The student's interests are then translated into goals for high school course work and post-secondary goals in four areas:

- **Education.** Goals for education include what the student wants to study in a post-secondary setting, where the student wants to study, admission requirements for the desired school and program, and associated financial obligations.
- **Training.** Training refers to specific skills necessary for desired employment, such as coding, equipment operation, food handling, interpersonal relations, or carpentry.
- **Employment.** Goals for employment focus on the student's desired trade or occupation. The target occupation may be available to the student immediately upon high school graduation or may require specific training or education.
- **Independent living.** Goals in this area relate to the type of housing the student desires upon completion of school as well as transportation necessary to access community services and activities.
- **Daily living skills.** Goals in this area include personal living skills such as cooking, eating, dressing, and grooming.

May I see some examples of IEP goals for transition?

Certainly. Here are some examples that might be useful.

1. Given eight persuasive reading selections, Starla will say and write the meaning of words and phrases as they are used in a text, including figurative, connotative, and technical meanings; and she will analyze and explain the cumulative impact of specific word choices on meaning and tone (e.g., how the language of a court opinion differs from that of a newspaper), 7/8 selections correct. (CCSA.ELA-literacy.RI.9-10.4)
   - This education goal addresses a Common Core reading for information standard that will prepare Starla to analyze and understand what she reads so she can protect herself from spurious print and online information and help her make good choices.
2. Using voice-activated dialing on a smartphone and with weekly practice in school and community settings, Isabella will call her mother to ask questions and report her location correctly in seven out of seven role-play scenarios.
   - This daily living skill goal will prepare Isabella to use a cell phone to stay in touch with her mother and ask for help if needed.

3. Given transportation to Valley Applied Technology Center, Alejandro will complete the first year of the plumbing apprenticeship by passing each course and assessment with mastery standards proficiency.
   - This is an employment goal meant to begin preparing Alejandro for good employment after graduation. Next year the goal would be to complete the second year of the two-year course.

How are post-school goals different from IEP goals?

Post-secondary goals are written on the transition plan and must clearly state that the behavior will occur *after* the student leaves school. The goals must be observable and pertain to employment, education or training, and independent living skills, if needed. Post-secondary goals must be directed toward realizing the student's personal ambitions and desires. Because the student will no longer be in K-12 school, no special educator will be responsible for monitoring progress toward or attainment of post-secondary goals, but the transition plan must manifestly be aimed at preparing the student to accomplish the goals after completing post-secondary schooling.

May I see some examples of post-secondary transition goals?

Yes. Look at these and see that they pertain to the student after leaving school, are measurable, and pertain to employment, education or training, or independent living. Notice they use the pattern (After high school, After completing school, Upon graduation, etc.) (student) will (observable behavior) (how or why) and (in what place).

1. After completing high school, Sarim will learn house framing by working in his uncle's local residential construction business.
   - This **training** goal tells when (after completing high school), the student (Sarim), the behavior (learn framing), how (by working with his uncle), in what place (local business).
2. After high school, Maran will learn transportation skills by participating in the city-sponsored program to help adults with disabilities learn to use the St. Regis City bus and light rail systems independently.
   - This **independent living** goal tells when (after high school), the student (Maran), the behavior (learn transportation skills), how, (participate in the city-sponsored program), in what place (St. Regis City).
3. Upon graduation, Astrid will prepare for work as a chairside assistant by enrolling in the dental assisting program at MedCareer Technical School.
   - This **education** goal tells when (upon graduation), the student (Astrid), the behavior (prepare for work as a chairside assistant), how (by enrolling in the dental assisting program), in what place (MedCareer Technical School).

TRANSITION SERVICES, INCLUDING COURSES OF STUDY, NECESSARY TO ASSIST THE STUDENT IN REACHING THE GOALS

The second step in transition planning is to determine what services must be provided during the school years to help the student reach the post-secondary goals. Because transition services may be provided outside the school, the team must invite a representative of any participating agency that will be responsible for providing or paying for transition services. Such agencies may include public or private job-training services, welfare services, mental health agencies, or other community-based programs.

Transition services may include any or all of the following:

- *Instruction*, including courses of study that address academic or skill-training preparation for achieving post-secondary goals
- *Related services* necessary for the student to achieve annual IEP goals
- *Community experiences* provided outside the school, such as community-based job exploration, job-site training, banking, shopping, transportation, health care, counseling, and recreation activities
- If appropriate, the acquisition of *daily living skills*, such as grooming, laundry care, food preparation, and budgeting.
- If appropriate, the provision of a *functional vocational evaluation* to determine the student's readiness for employment. This involves a comprehensive assessment of the student's vocational preferences and skills to work in both general and specific work settings. The evaluation can be accomplished with formal or informal assessments of the student's strengths, aptitudes, interests, work experiences, and other relevant attributes.

How about some examples of transition services for Starla, Isabella, Sarim, and Maran?

Here are our suggestions:

- Starla will enroll in and complete a tenth-grade English class that teaches reading for information.
- Isabella will receive instruction in her classroom and practice in various places in the school and community accompanied by her special education teacher.
- Sarim will receive instruction to achieve competency in linear measurement, fractions, and angles.
- Maran will master stating his purpose for transportation, asking questions, and following directions.

A STATEMENT THAT THE STUDENT HAS BEEN INFORMED OF THE TRANSFER OF ADULT RIGHTS NO LATER THAN ONE YEAR BEFORE THE STUDENT REACHES THE AGE OF MAJORITY

The third requirement for transition planning is to inform the student of the pending transfer of adult rights to the student at the age of legal adult status in the state of residence, unless the student is deemed incompetent to assume adult rights (§300.520 (a)). This requirement must be completed no later than one year *before* the student reaches the age of majority, which differs from state to state. Check with your local school or district to see if a special form is used for this process.

SUMMARY OF PERFORMANCE

IDEA requires schools to summarize the academic achievement and functional performance of students with disabilities who graduate or who no longer receive special education after age 22. The school must provide a copy of the summary to the student. This summary of performance should provide enough information so that the individual can meet disability qualification standards for the *Americans with Disabilities Act* and other laws pertinent to adults with disabilities.

MAY I SEE AN EXAMPLE OF A TRANSITION PLAN?

Most assuredly. Look at Keej's transition plan appended to his IEP. You will find each requirement addressed on the form.

MY MENTOR — Note that the IEP and the transition plan are complementary documents, and IEP teams serve secondary students most effectively when IEP goals are addressed with educational services as well as community-based services.

YOUR TURN

Select the service(s) your IEP team would recommend for Josh, a 17-year-old adolescent with orthopedic impairments, in order to meet the annual goal listed below. Check your answers with our suggestions in the Appendix.

ANNUAL GOAL

When Josh arrives at work from the city bus, he will independently wheel himself into the building, clock in, and begin his work, with no verbal prompts, for at least four weeks.

Services:

☐ Training ☐ Education ☐ Employment

☐ Independent Living ☐ Daily Living Skills

Congratulations! You have learned and practiced all seven steps for writing quality IEPs. Now you should be ready to serve on a team of parents and professionals who are committed to serving all students with disabilities in an ethical and professional manner. With some practical experience, you will become comfortable writing quality IEPs.

Transition Resources

Center for Parent Information and Resources www.parentcenterhub.org

Division on Career Development and Transition https://community.cec.sped.org/dcdt/home

IDEA Partnership www.ideapartnership.org

National Center on Secondary Education and Transition www.ncset.org

National Secondary Transition Technical Assistance Center www.transitionta.org

Ticket to Work for adults with disabilities https://choosework.ssa.gov

Answers to Exercises

STEP 1

Example PLAAFP for Samuel

Samuel can do one-digit addition and subtraction without renaming, but cannot add or subtract multiple digits without renaming and cannot multiply and divide. He can dictate simple sentences when given a subject, but cannot compose and write simple sentences when given a subject. He can identify his backpack, but cannot place school materials in the backpack when directed. He can use the restroom independently, but cannot fasten pants or wash hands before leaving the restroom. He can follow two-step requests in order, but he does not wait his turn in line; he can talk with his friends, but interrupts others in their conversations. To progress in the general curriculum, Samuel needs to use place value understanding and properties of operations to perform multi-digit arithmetic (CCSS.MATH. CONTENT.4.NBT.B). Additionally, with guidance and support from peers and adults he should develop and strengthen writing as needed by planning, revising, and editing (CCSS.ELA-LITERACY.W.4.5), and he needs to improve self-help and socialization skills.

Error in Kingston's PLAAFP

This PLAAFP entry provides a "can do" statement but no "cannot" or "does not do" statement. A more specific statement would require additional information related to this skill: for example, "Lance initiates and sustains conversations with peers and can call his friends on the telephone. He does not ask his teacher for assistance when needed. He does not distinguish between appropriate and inappropriate comments to female peers."

Error in Evangeline's PLAAFP

This statement provides information unrelated to Evangeline's disability, which is in reading, not penmanship. A better statement would require specific information about her reading skills: for example, "Evangeline has mastered kindergarten reading standards. She cannot decode words or read fluently at the grade level."

Error in McCoy's PLAAFP

McCoy's statement provides a vague description of McCoy's social/behavioral skills. A more descriptive PLAAFP would require specific information about his social/behavioral skills, such as "When directed to engage in work-related tasks, McCoy throws his school materials and yells at the teacher an average of eight times per day. He complains daily that he does not like school. McCoy's behavior interferes with his progress in the general academic and social curriculum."

STEP 2

PLAAFP Statement for Maddie

Conditions	Behavior	Criteria	Generalization	Maintenance
When given a grocery list with five or fewer items and a $10.00 bill	Maddie will select and purchase	all the items on the list with fewer than five prompts	in three different grocery stores	over a three-week period

PLAAFP Statement for Suraj

Conditions	Behavior	Criteria	Generalization	Maintenance
When directed by the teacher to be seated	Suraj will sit quietly at his desk	within five seconds, 90% of instances	in each of his classes	over a four-week period.

Benjamin's Benchmarks

When presented with 10 items and asked to count them, Benjamin will point to and orally count the items correctly with no prompts.

PERFORMANCE
1. *Benchmark:* In 10 weeks when presented with 10 items and asked to count them, Benjamin will point to and orally count the items with at least 50% accuracy.
2. *Benchmark:* In 20 weeks when presented with 10 items and asked to count them, Benjamin will point to and orally count the items with at least 80% accuracy.

ASSISTANCE LEVEL
1. *Benchmark:* In 10 weeks when presented with 10 items and asked to count them, Benjamin will point to and orally count the items correctly with verbal prompts, 10/10 correct.
2. *Benchmark:* In 20 weeks when presented with 10 items and asked to count them, Benjamin will point to and orally count the items correctly with no prompts, 10/10 correct.

TASK ANALYSIS

1. *Benchmark:* In 10 weeks when presented with five items and asked to count them, Benjamin will point and orally count the items correctly with no prompts, 5/5 correct.
2. *Benchmark:* In 20 weeks when presented with 10 items and asked to count them, Benjamin will point to and orally count the items correctly with no prompts, 10/10 correct.

GENERALIZATION

1. *Benchmark:* In 10 weeks when presented with 10 identical items and asked to count them, Benjamin will point to and orally count the items correctly with no prompts, 10/10 correct.
2. *Benchmark:* In 20 weeks when presented with 10 dissimilar items and asked to count them, Benjamin will point to and orally count the items correctly with no prompts, 10/10 correct.

Benjamin's Short-Term Objectives

1. *Short-term objective:* When presented with 10 items and asked to point to each, Benjamin will point to each item, 10/10 correct, 3/3 consecutive trials.
2. *Short-term objective:* When presented with 10 items and asked to point to and orally count them, Benjamin will point to and orally count all items, 10/10 correct, 3/3 consecutive trials.

STEP 3
Measuring Mikiah's Goal

MEASUREMENT METHOD

☐ formal assessment   ☐ criterion referenced   ☐ curriculum-based

☒ skills checklist   ☐ behavior observation   ☐ work sample

RATIONALE

An informal teacher checklist will allow the teacher to track progress as the student demonstrates mastery of each component of the skill.

Measuring Alonzo's Goal

MEASUREMENT METHOD

☐ formal assessment ☐ criterion referenced ☒ curriculum-based

☐ skills checklist ☐ behavior observation ☐ work sample

RATIONALE

The criteria require Alonzo to write answers, so an informal curriculum-based measure with 10 items for each operation is most appropriate.

STEP 4

Services for Cadence

1. What special education services does Cadence require?
   - *Specially designed instruction in both regular and special class settings*
2. What related services does Cadence require?
   - *Speech-language services*
3. What supplementary aids and services in the regular classroom does Cadence require?
   - *Paraeducator in general education classroom*
4. What program modifications and supports do Cadence's teachers require?
   - *Support training and consultation for teacher and paraeducators*
5. What special factors did the IEP team choose?
   - *Communication and/or language services*
6. Explain why you think the team recommended these services.
   - *Each of these aids and services are required for Cadence to achieve her IEP goals.*

STEP 5

Boston's Statement of Nonparticipation

The student will participate in the regular class, extracurricular, and nonacademic activities except as noted here: *Boston will receive physical therapy and adaptive P.E during regular P.E. time. One class period each week (so he isn't totally excluded from PE, but still gets individualized services.)*

Asher's Statement of Nonparticipation

The student will participate in the regular class, extracurricular, and nonacademic activities except as noted here: *Not applicable*

STEP 6

Amara's Accommodation

Dictate answers to scribe.

Derrick's Accommodation

Provide large-print materials or provide magnification equipment.

Kalappan's Accommodation

Take tests in study carrel or take test in room with three or fewer students.

Duong's Modification

Teacher reads aloud reading subtests; student answers comprehension questions orally.

Novia's Modification

Provide more breaks than allowed by test publisher, or reduce number of test items.

Ezzie's Suggested Assessment

Alternate assessment

Aisha's Suggested Assessment

Alternate assessment

STEP 7

Josh's Transition IEP Goal Services

☒	Training	*Josh may need training to achieve this goal.*
☐	Education	*This is a job-related goal; post-secondary education is not mentioned.*
☒	Employment	*Josh needs a job in order to achieve this goal.*
☒	Independent living	*Josh needs transportation to get to his work site.*
☐	Daily living skills	*This a job-related goal; daily living skills are not mentioned.*

Text Credits

Meet Our Students (MOS)

Excerpt from CCSS.ELA-Literacy.RF.2.3. © Copyright 2010 National Governors Association Center for Best Practices and Council of Chief State School Officers. All rights reserved. (Pages 26, 31.)

Excerpt from CCSS.MATH.CONTENT.8.EE.C.8.C. © Copyright 2010 National Governors Association Center for Best Practices and Council of Chief State School Officers. All rights reserved. (Page 31.)

Excerpt from CCSS.ELA-Literacy.RF.5.4. © Copyright 2010 National Governors Association Center for Best Practices and Council of Chief State School Officers. All rights reserved. (Pages 31, 32.)

Step 2

National Governors Association Center for Best Practices, Council of Chief State School Officers. (2010). Common Core State Standards. Washington, DC. Available at http://www.corestandards.org (Page 70.)

Step 3

National Governors Association Center for Best Practices, Council of Chief State School Officers. (2010). Common Core State Standards. Washington, DC. Available at http://www.corestandards.org (Page 88.)

Step 4

National Governors Association Center for Best Practices, Council of Chief State School Officers. (2010). Common Core State Standards. Washington, DC. Available at http://www.corestandards.org (Page 94.)

Step 7

National Governors Association Center for Best Practices, Council of Chief State School Officers. (2010). Common Core State Standards. Washington, DC. Available at http://www.corestandards.org (Page 123.)

Appendix

National Governors Association Center for Best Practices, Council of Chief State School Officers. (2010). Common Core State Standards. Washington, DC. Available at http://www.corestandards.org (Page 128.)